SUCCESSFUL
PREDATOR
HUNTING

MICHAEL SCHOBY

Published by

kp books
An Imprint of F+W Publications

700 East State Street • Iola, WI 54990-0001
715-445-2214 • 888-457-2873

Please call for our free catalog. Our toll-free number to place an order or obtain a free catalog is 800-258-0929 or please use our regular business telephone 715-445-2214 .

Library of Congress Catalog Number: 2003105286
ISBN: 0-87349-544-6
Printed in the United States of America

Dedication

To my father, who started me along the outdoor trail.

Table of Contents

Foreword

I believe that all of us who are hunters dream of hunting strange and magnificent creatures in the far-flung corners of the globe: animals such as grizzly, Cape buffalo, wild sheep, greater kudu; places with exotic names like Yukon, Serengeti, Pamir, and Kalahari. Some of us are fortunate enough to realize some of these dreams, but it really doesn't matter. We are all hunters. Despite our dreams and desires, and whether or not we are able to make some of them come true, most of us spend the majority of our precious time afield hunting game that is most available in our own backyards.

It has always been so. In the 1920s, my Kansas-born grandfather hunted the vast numbers of waterfowl that traded down the Kansas and Missouri rivers. The "dust bowl" of the 1930s followed years of uncontrolled market hunting, and the stream of ducks dwindled to a slow trickle. My grandfather became an upland bird hunter. My father was raised hunting quail and pheasants over good bird dogs. So was I, 20 years later. But things changed again. Farming got cleaner and bigger, and many of the brushy hedgerows and streambeds disappeared – and as the human population increased and good upland bird habitat grew more scarce, "no hunting" signs became ever more prevalent.

During this same period, many of the new impoundments and reservoirs matured, and conservation efforts brought back the waterfowl – geese in unprecedented numbers, and more ducks than any member of my generation had ever seen. My quail and pheasant hunting buddies got duck boats, decoys and retrievers and became waterfowl hunters. The whitetail population exploded as well, and these same hunters whose fathers had never owned centerfire rifles became deer hunters, and today can argue the virtues of .270s and .300 magnums just as well as they could discuss the advantages of over/unders versus semiautos and pumps a couple of decades earlier.

So what does all this have to do with varmint hunting and, more specifically, predator hunting? Hunters are hunters, and nationwide, most of them will always hunt the game that's most available closest to home. Across the country right now, opportunity to hunt varmints is not only at an all-time high, but for many of us represents the class of game that is most plentiful, most available, and most affordable. There are many reasons for this. Pluses for the varmints include cessation of poisoning as a means of control; and, for furbearers, cessation of trapping and an all-time low in fur prices. These have led to booms in predator populations. Coyotes are now found from coast to coast, and fox and bobcat populations are also burgeoning. Black bears, classed as big game with resultant protection, are rapidly increasing in both population and range. Cougars are as well.

For the hunter, this translates into opportunity, with some extra pluses as well. Unlike big game, upland game and waterfowl, in most areas seasons for predators and other varmints are long (often year-'round), and hunting licenses (if required at all) are basic and inexpensive. Bag limits are generally nonexistent. Of course, in this day and age one of the real keys to hunting is a place to hunt. This is also much simpler for varmints than for any other class of game. Farmers and ranchers who wouldn't consider allowing access for deer or upland game are often downright grateful to have predator callers and prairie dog and 'chuck shooters on their lands. In fact, with poisoning and trapping a thing of the past, varmint hunters are now the single most important tools for maintaining predator and rodent populations in an acceptable balance.

As you will see in this book, there is an extensive range of equipment that *might* be used in predator hunting: sophisticated calls, specialized rifles, decoys, portable blinds, night vision devices, and more. If used (and always, if used *correctly*), such equipment offers an advantage and probably adds to both success and enjoyment. But the actual requirements for successful varmint hunting are actually very simple: an inexpensive mouth-

blown call, a reasonably appropriate firearm, basic camouflage and a bit of knowledge. Compare this to the dogs, decoys, boats, blinds and duck leases serious waterfowlers find essential today.

In the 1920s and 1930s, when big-game populations were at their nadir, varmint hunting was an extremely popular sport in many parts of the country. In my younger days, it was considered primarily an "off-season" pastime. For many it still is, but for the reasons mentioned above – availability, access, affordability – today there is an unprecedented interest in varminting, with growing numbers of sportsmen and women considering it their primary hunting focus, interrupted only by short seasons for other game.

Michael Schoby is just enough younger than I am (lucky guy!) that this is the world he came into as a hunter. Growing up in Washington's Cascades, he had the benefit of excellent (but short) seasons for deer and elk. But as a teenager he recognized that his best hunting opportunity (available, accessible, affordable) was offered by the plentiful predators in his neighborhood – not only coyotes and bobcats, but black bears and cougars as well. He was 14 when he called in his first coyote, and in the many years since has remained fascinated by the tactics, techniques and downright excitement involved with hunting predators. As he told me, "There were several years in my early 20s when I hunted predators year 'round and nothing else."

As a hunter, he has realized some of those dreams we all have – but even in Africa's Drakensberg Mountains and Kalahari Desert, he couldn't resist the urge to take out his varmint call and bring in jackals and African lynx. He is a charter member of America's growing group of *serious* predator hunters, a student of the art and an aficionado of the sport.

I freely admit that I am not nearly so serious about predator hunting – certainly not to the exclusion of all else – but I have dabbled heavily in it for many years and in many places. In reading Michael's book (which, in no way would I be qualified to write), I can say that I agree with almost all of his recommendations and conclusions. I don't know if this should be considered flattery or an expression of ignorance on my part, so I'll go a step further: I learned a great deal from an initial reading, and I look forward to learning more as I really study his tactics and techniques and relate them to successes and failures I've had in the past. If you enjoy predator hunting, you will enjoy this book, and in comparing his views against your own experience, you will probably disagree here and there, you will find some of your own tactics validated and you will almost certainly learn a few tricks. If you are new to the game, you will also enjoy this book – and you will learn a great deal.

In the past, my primary interaction with Michael Schoby has been in my role as a writer and his role as an editor. I have admired the articles he has written, and I have come to respect him as that rarity in our business – a truly competent editor who is also a serious hunter. But in this work, I have now seen an altogether different side of this still-young man: In the world of predator hunting, he is truly an expert. He has a bright future in our business, and I suspect there will be many more years of articles and books under his byline. Whether this comes to pass or not, *Successful Predator Hunting* can stand alone as a truly authoritative work on the subject. You'll like it as much as I do!

Craig Boddington
Camp Doha, Kuwait
December 2002

Acknowledgments

I am typing this from my home in western Nebraska on a prime winter predator hunting night. The moon is full, and there isn't even the slightest hint of a breeze. I should be out hunting. However, I have put this last part of my book off until I have no other choice than to just finish it. It is relatively simple to write about hunting predators; it is not so simple trying to find the right words to thank the individuals who helped me complete a project that took the better part of a year.

Where does one begin with acknowledgments? So many people have helped me with this project, it is hard to know where to start. The first person who comes to mind is my father, Paul Schoby. Weekly I sent chapters to him for initial editing, and each week chapters returned, covered in red, blue and green marks. His editing skills are excellent, and even though some stung (as all good editing should), he improved the final work tremendously. Thank you, dad, for all the work (and mom for helping him figure out the computer). Without it, this book would never have been published.

To the many hunting partners I have shared a sunrise with, thanks for tolerating my time-consuming and often annoying photo sessions. In particular, thank you Mike Lunenschloss, Taro Sakita, Mark Mazour, Darrin Fehringer and Mark Boardman. The times we have shared afield have always been enjoyable.

There comes a time in every book when it needs professional help, and mine was no exception. Thanks to Craig Boddington, Thomas McIntyre, Mitch Kezar, Gary Kramer and Bill Bynum. All took time from their busy schedules and helped with editorial material, interviews and photo support. Thank you again. I appreciate it tremendously.

I think that covers almost everyone, but I am sure I missed a few. If you are one of those people, remind me and I will remember you in my next book. But for now, I think it's time to shut down for the night and head afield for a couple of stands while the moon is still high.

Thanks again and good hunting,

Michael Schoby

1

Predator Hunting – Past, Present and Future

Predator hunting has been with us for a very long time. "Riding to the hounds" has been a sport of the elite in Europe for centuries. In my father's youth, fox drives and tracking on fresh snow were popular weekend activities of neighboring farmers in rural Indiana. One even had a light airplane he used to locate bedded foxes for ground hunters to pursue. Most hunters took potshots at coyotes and foxes in passing, and nearly every rancher had a rifle in the pickup or behind the kitchen door for the "vermin."

Predator hunting as we know and understand it today was in its very early infancy 50 years ago. An occasional article would appear in a magazine. A handful of people were tinkering with calls, but the average hunter didn't pay much attention. Almost nothing was available in the way of specialized equipment. Very few people considered predator hunting a "sport" in itself. There were exceptions. Murray Burnham and Johnny Stewart down in Texas, and Bert Poposki up in the Dakotas were dedicated predator hunters. Still, serious predator hunters were far from numerous. These pioneers were ahead of their time, but they knew the secret: Predators are fun to hunt and are often the most exciting and challenging game available.

In recent years, predator hunting has gone through an enormous evolution. Fantastic advances in equipment and material have been made. Techniques have been refined. Availability and distribution of information has increased. Publicity and interest has exploded. Even the range and populations of the quarry have expanded.

Predators are fun to hunt, and they're often the most exciting and challenging game available.

Coyotes prey on livestock and other farm animals when given the chance. No wonder ranchers want them thinned from their property.

expanding. No wonder the popularity of predator hunting is growing rapidly.

Why Hunt Predators?

The natural world will always be regulated by the balance between predator and prey. In most places, however, this balance has been altered through human encroachment, destruction of natural habitat and other artificial influences. All game species from grouse to elk are managed by game biologists to the carrying capacity of the land. This is a good thing and ensures a continuing supply of game animals for us to hunt. But predators have also responded to this increase in the food base and not only take their share of game animals, but often encroach on non-game species and domestic livestock.

Next to habitat loss, predation is the biggest variable that affects game populations. This is true for species as small as rabbits and as large as elk. In Washington's Blue Mountains, for instance, elk numbers have been declining in recent years due to increased predation on elk calves by cougars and bears. The Washington Department of Fish and Wildlife has deemed that a higher harvest of predators increases the elk population.

Aside from scientific reasons for predator hunting, there is a human factor that's hard to ignore. Gaining access to private lands for big game or bird hunting has become very difficult in most parts of the country.

Landowners across the U.S. are concerned about the liabilities and nuisance factor of allowing access to their property. A hunter might get injured and sue the landowner, or he might be a "slob" who leaves gates open, gets stuck, accidentally shoots livestock or equipment, or even vandalizes equipment. Today, there are many serious disadvantages, and no advantages, for a landowner to allow free hunting on his property.

But there's a rub. Many farmers and ranchers would like predators thinned from their property, but they are often too busy to hunt them. Most of the time, this hunting opportunity is there for the asking. It's a great way to meet landowners and prove your merit as an ethical, safe hunter and develop a good relationship.

These days, more and more people hunt for the challenge of it rather than to put food on the table. Hopefully, filling the larder with game will always play a big part in why we hunt, but our survival no longer depends on it. Consequently, we hunt for many other reasons, from experiencing nature to the challenge of the pursuit, to mutual enjoyment and camaraderie. For those who thrive on matching wits with wild animals, nothing beats hunting predators. They are stealthy, smart hunters themselves, and it takes skill to bag one. If whitetails were treated like coyotes and could be hunted year-round, day or night, with no regard to bag limits or methods, what would happen? Very quickly the deer population would plummet, as it did during the market hunting days of the late 1800s.

Opportunistic feeders, coyotes prey on a wide variety of animals – game and non-game species alike.

The coyote's natural wariness, keen sense of smell and other sharp senses are what make them so difficult to hunt.

Predator hunting is one of the best ways to gain access to private lands, and often leads to other hunting opportunities.

Today, there are many hunting videos, several books and at least two magazines dedicated to – you guessed it – predator hunting. We've suddenly gone from incidental predator shooters to dedicated predator hunters.

Why all the change? There are many reasons. Increased predator numbers have played a significant role. Not long ago, government funding of damage control officers was greater than it is today. In addition, pelt prices were substantially higher, and most forms of poison were completely legal. Bounties were also paid on many species, some of which are now protected. Today, in our politically correct world, the government predator men are seldom talked about, and their numbers are few indeed. Fur prices are so low that trapping has dwindled. Ranchers may now face prosecution for poisoning predators. Severe restrictions on trapping, baiting and pursuit with dogs have been enacted in many states. All of these factors have caused predator numbers to rise. In some cases, it has skipped the "rise" and has gone straight through the roof!

There's also much more information and gear than ever before. Until recently, only a few hunters knew how to consistently bring predators to a call. Others had heard it could be done, but did not attempt it for a lack of knowledge. Today, a beginner can readily find instructions or even personal help to get started.

As big-game hunting opportunities wane in many areas, most predator hunting opportunities are

Hunting coyotes is a good way to keep your hunting skills sharp year-round.

When wolves were driven out of their historic Western range, coyotes moved in to take their place. Coyotes now range from coast to coast and have been discovered inside many major metropolitan areas including New York City.

However, the situation just described fits the policy on coyotes in most states. But instead of dwindling in number, coyotes have thrived and expanded their territory to regions where they haven't been since colonial times.

What about the harvest numbers? Coyotes taken incidentally while hunting other game or even by the novice predator hunter per year, per hunter, can often be counted on one hand with several fingers left over. A serious predator hunter may bag 50 coyotes per year – and an extremely proficient hunter may take more – but this is rare and takes full dedication to the sport. It just goes to show how difficult predators are to take and how seldom hunters are successful.

Extending your hunting days is another reason to take up predator hunting. In most states, modern rifle hunters who do not capitalize on late seasons, bonus tags or primitive-weapon seasons spend an average of two weeks hunting whitetails. Granted, in some states, deer seasons are substantially longer than two weeks, but many are as short as one week in other locales. Even if you are fortunate enough to live in a state that allows a month of modern rifle season, that leaves another 11 months to dream about hunting. Predator hunting allows you to stay afield most of the year. If you find yourself itching to pick up a rifle and head outdoors in the off-season, don't overlook predators. The opportunities are nearly unlimited.

Since most big-game hunters only venture afield for a weekend or two each year, it should be no surprise that many are less than proficient with their chosen firearm, gear and woodsmanship. Any time spent hunting predators will always improve our skills for other forms of hunting. Predator hunters become more proficient with their firearms and other gear, increase their powers of observation and gain a better understanding of the natural environment game animals inhabit. If you hunt in rough terrain, this extra time will also help keep you in shape for long hikes after bigger game.

Finally, one of the biggest advantages I glean from predator hunting, other than the pure enjoyment of the sport itself, is the scouting I get while doing it. Many times while hunting coyotes, I have found a great turkey spot, a deer hideout, a hidden bass pond or even a mushroom patch. I tuck this information away and put it to good use sometime in the future. If it wasn't for exploration while predator hunting, these spots would still remain unknown to me.

Photo by Gary Kramer.

The howl of a coyote is a symbol of the wild, and it would be a lonely place without it.

Ethics and Sportsmanship

"They're only coyotes."

"It doesn't matter how you kill them as long as you do."

"Shoot them all if you get a chance."

I have heard all of these statements over the years, some uttered by landowners, others by so-called "sportsmen." For whatever reason, predators have earned little respect among outdoor types. As hunters, we're probably not going to change such long-held opinions overnight, but that doesn't mean we shouldn't respect our quarry. All predators have their place in the natural order of things and serve a vital function. Why would anyone want to eliminate predators, anyway? The world would be a much sadder place without the bark and yip of a song dog closing the day, or the howl of a wolf or the sighting of an elusive cougar. These animals are our last link to the wildness of nature and which by design we are a part of.

Respect for the Sport, Respect for the Quarry

Every wild creature, even those we set out to kill, deserves the respect of ethical hunters. This includes the rules of fair chase, humane treatment in terms of methods and seasons, maximum utilization and good taste in display and disposal.

As with any game, take only shots that ensure a quick and clean kill. Pass up shots at long ranges and at running animals. A wounded or lost animal will be the likely result. Botched opportunities also result in an alerted animal that will be more difficult to approach or attract later. Use a cartridge adequate for the job and a gun that's properly sighted. Practice with it enough that you can shoot it well.

Don't take animals during the denning season or with dependent young. No animal deserves to starve in the den or perish from parental neglect.

Use judgment and good taste when transporting and displaying your kill. The sight of a dead animal, even a predator, is offensive to many people. It makes no sense to invite their criticism.

Make maximum use of the harvest. Predator pelts provide a beautiful and valuable fur that shouldn't be wasted. Teeth and claws make interesting early-American necklaces and jewelry. Most of the small predators are not generally considered for human consumption. However, bears are certainly edible. In fact, game laws in many areas require that bear meat be brought out of the woods for use and not be allowed to go to waste. The raw flesh is fine-textured and light in color, but darkens considerably when cooked and loses some of its eye appeal. It makes wonderful salami or summer sausage. I have it on good authority from an old friend and lifetime resident of western Washington that cougar is one of the finest of all wild meats. I have not tried it, but on his endorsement would not hesitate if given the opportunity. The meat of any wild carnivore or omnivore such as bears or swine should be thoroughly cooked. There could be risk of trichinosis, although I don't know of any specific cases.

Finally, dispose of the remains of any animal in a remote place well out of sight of those who would criticize. Pick a spot where it can gently return to the nutrients of the earth and nourish nature's wonderful cycle.

2

Coyotes East and West

Coyotes are the most common predator in the United States. Challenging to hunt and beautiful to behold, they are the predator's predator.

Photo by David Draper

C oyotes are one of America's premier success stories (or failures, depending upon your point of view). They have been shot, poisoned, chased (from aircraft, car and snowmobile) and trapped. Bounties on these animals have been in place in various states since 1825, and government-paid predator control officers are still on the job today. Through all of this, coyotes have thrived where other species would have become endangered or extinct. Once thought of as only a Western species, coyotes now range from coast to coast and have been discovered inside the city limits of many major metropolitan centers, including New York and Seattle.

Mice, rats or rabbits? It doesn't matter to a hungry coyote, an equal-opportunity feeder.

Key to Survival

Two factors have ensured the coyote's survival and expansion over the last couple of hundred years. Before pioneers began settling the West, the coyote's range was restricted to the open plains and arid deserts. Wolves dominated the forests and mountains. With Manifest Destiny and the development of Western ranching and farming, the wolf was slowly eradicated from the lower 48. This came about through the destruction of much of its forage base (namely big game) and human encroachment. As the wolf adapted to the new big game of the plains – primarily cattle and sheep – it quickly fell out of grace with local ranchers trying to eke out a living from the harsh land. Hunting pressure from ranchers, farmers and bounty hunters subsequently drove the wolf to the most remote reaches of its range.

As this prime niche opened up, coyotes established a stronger foothold. What they were given was nothing more than an opportunity to survive. And survive they did, owing largely to their diverse diet. Simply put, coyotes can and do eat anything they can fit down their throat. Rodents, fish, amphibians, rabbits, sheep, fawns, calves, watermelon, corn, carrion, birds, garbage – all are considered an epicurean delight to a hungry coyote. With such a varied and undiscerning palate, it's no wonder these animals had no trouble living anywhere in the U.S. once given the chance.

While a coyote's diet usually consists of rodents, rabbits and birds, they also feast on large game animals and domestic stock.

The Western Plains is the original home of *Canis Latrans*.

Coyote Biology

Coyotes are members of the Canidae family, specifically *Canis latrans* (meaning barking dog), which includes dogs, foxes, wolves and jackals. A male coyote averages between 44 and 52 inches long and weighs between 25 and 40 pounds. Depending upon whom you talk to, there are between 15 to 21 coyote subspecies. To a wildlife biologist, these are discernable, but the average sportsman knows of only two major subspecies: the Eastern coyote and the Western coyote, also called prairie coyote. Coyotes in the Eastern U.S. are typically much larger than their Western cousins and weigh between 40 and 50 pounds.

Hunting East to West

One cannot talk about coyote hunting without mentioning the differences between the Eastern and Western subspecies. The mighty Mississippi is more than a delineation line of the country; it also separates coyotes. Eastern and Western coyotes not only differ in size, but also in "personality." Eastern coyote habitat is largely a mixture of hardwood forests, river systems and agricultural land. In the West, vast open prairies are the norm, complete with deserts, huge mountain ranges and some river systems. Western coyotes have to cover more territory to secure a meal. The arid country simply doesn't supply much forage per acre, and skittish jackrabbits and

During the last 100 years, coyotes have expanded their range across the U.S. They now thrive despite intensive campaigns to control or eliminate them in ranching areas.

Coyote scat is easy to distinguish by its unique shape and some-times-unusual content matter.

A typical coyote track in sandy soil. Note the track's elongated length and sharp claw indentations.

a scattering of mice are typical coyote fare. In Eastern farming country, small rodents, game birds and rabbits abound. Hunting areas are smaller but food-rich.

Eastern coyotes are also believed to be more nocturnal than their Western cousins. Whether this is due to greater human contact or not is hard to say, but it appears to be the case. Expect to call most Eastern coyotes in the extreme early-morning and late-evening hours. Cottontail rabbits are the main food staple, so most hunters choose a high-pitched cottontail-in-distress call over the coarser jackrabbit call. Eastern hunters should also be prepared to call in smaller patches of country, mostly farm fields surrounded by hardwood trees. In this kind of environment, visibility is limited, making it easy for a coyote to sneak downwind of the caller's position. Choose your stand site carefully and have a hunting partner positioned to cover the back door. Since Eastern coyotes usually don't come to the call from extreme long distances, I generally don't call as long or as loud as I do out West. Further, in the East, I don't move as far before making another calling stand.

Of course, agricultural land also exists in the West, and hunting in such places can be very similar to that in the East. But in stereotypical Western landscapes – vast open plains covered in either grass stands or sagebrush, occasionally broken up by rimrocked canyons and basalt cliffs – hunting is very different. Due to the distinct lack of trees in the open Western landscape, sound travels a long way. Prey species are also fewer here. For both of these reasons, Western coyotes tend to travel long distances when coming to a call – a mile or more is not out of the question if a coyote is in the mood. Both cottontail and jackrabbit calls work, so call selection is not much of a concern. Expect to take longer shots here, too; cover is sparse in many Western locales, so coyotes often hold up instead of coming all the way in.

Coyote Sign

Coyotes tend to leave a lot of sign, and it's usually easy to determine if they're in an area. Look for scat along well-used trails, which they deposit as a sort of territorial marker. Unlike cats, coyotes do not cover their scat with dirt. A large amount of scat along a trail or fence corner indicates a reasonably high coyote population and should be considered a prime calling location.

Coyote scat is generally doglike in appearance and tapered at both ends. However, unlike the scat of a dog, it usually is full of all sorts of strange material. Fur, bone fragments and berry seeds are the most common contents. This not only helps you distinguish it from dog feces, it also gives you an indication of what the animal has been feeding on.

Tracks are also common in a productive area, provided the ground is soft enough to print them. Coyote tracks appear similar to those of a dog's, but are much thinner, shorter and more tapered. The presence of their non-retractable claws is also evident, separating them from the round but similar pads of bobcats.

Gearing Up

I've been asked many times, "What gear do I need to get into coyote hunting?" While there are several chapters in this book that will possibly convince you that you need this or that, the answer is really simple: Coyote hunting is one of the easiest, most cost-effective hunting sports to get into. When I started, I had no specialized clothing, no optics, one call (retail price today $7.99) and a hand-me-down deer rifle. With this meager equipment, I shot more than a few coyotes. Once you decide you're really serious about hunting coyotes, the sky (as well as your wallet) is the limit to how much gear you can amass. While neither option is probably the right choice for the fledgling pred-

The author at age 14. No camo, no optics and a borrowed deer rifle. You can hunt coyotes with just the bare essentials, but some gear does make it easier.

Coyotes have been taken with almost every caliber in existence – in this case, a Westley Richards .416 Rigby. Enough gun for sure, but a .223 also works just fine.

ator hunter, here is what I would suggest a beginner should acquire:

• An accurate predator rifle – This doesn't have to be expensive. There are some extremely accurate and very affordable single-shot, break-open guns being produced strictly for predator hunting.

• A quality set of binoculars – While good optics may not be an absolute necessity, they will definitely help you bag more critters. Coyotes blend in very well with their surroundings, and a good pair of binoculars goes a long way at picking them out.

• Two calls – Calls are cheap, and you should own at least a couple. I like to carry a simple closed-reed call and either a bulb-type or an open-reed call in the eventuality that the closed-reed call freezes up in cold weather.

As you can see, getting geared up is a simple affair. If coyote hunting becomes your passion, there are literally hundreds of items that will keep you warmer, make you more effective and help you enjoy the sport more.

Finding a Hunting Place

So you've decided that you want to hunt coyotes, and you've rounded up some gear. Now what? Luckily for most hunters across the U.S., there's a huntable population of coyotes within a half-hour drive of their house. Start by looking for sign such as scat and tracks and lis-

A .243 Winchester is an ideal Western cartridge for coyotes when the wind blows and the ranges increase.

Coyotes are nothing if not stealthy. Watching one hunt is a sight to behold.

Photo by Gary Kramer

tening for howling activity around sunup and sundown. Good public places to begin searching are state game management areas, BLM land and national forests, as coyotes usually receive little pressure from other hunters.

Want to find private land to hunt? It's almost always free for the asking. In farming and ranching communities, landowners want coyotes removed from their property. Start knocking on doors and asking politely. You'll be amazed how much property will be opened up to you.

Calling Them In

The actual technique of calling coyotes is covered in much greater detail in other chapters of this book, but here are some thoughts specifically tailored to coyotes:

In my opinion, coyotes are the easiest of all of North America's predator species to call. They have the advantage of being fast, fearless of other animals (if a large population of bears or mountain lions occur in the same area, this is not always the case) and usually hungry. Combine these three factors, and you have a predator that responds well to a call. However, that's not to say they're stupid. Coyotes are born with an innate fear of man and are extremely wary. Everything must be done right if you expect to succeed.

Rule No. 1 of coyote hunting is to respect the animal's nose. Like other canines, coyotes have a well-developed sense of smell and often use it to their advantage when

approaching a call.

Set up in an area that's difficult for a coyote to approach from the downwind side. Large, steep gullies, rocky cliffs and even a plowed dirt field can help in funneling a coyote's movements and keeping the wind to your advantage. If the natural lay of the land does not allow you to control the animal's movements, set up another hunter 50 to 100 yards downwind of the your calling position to pick up the ones that circle around the back door for a sniff.

Coyote Rifles and Calibers

For a dedicated Western coyote rifle, I believe an accurate, fast-handling, bolt-action rifle chambered in .223, .22-250 or .243 is ideal. Most called coyotes are shot within 100 yards, and if the occasional long shot presents itself, any of these calibers has the gumption to do it. If you're hunting in an area known for wind or are forced to take shots a tad on the long side, opt for a .243 Winchester. The heavier bullets drift less in the wind and have the added advantage of carrying more energy downrange.

In the East, where shots are generally taken at shorter ranges, I would still use a fast-handling bolt-action rifle, but would consider the .223 on the large side for calibers. The .223 has more then enough authority to anchor any

For a dedicated predator hunter, coyotes are the meat and potatoes of the sport. Few ever get tired of hunting them.

coyote when loaded with the right bullets and kept within its effective range. If urban sprawl or nearby farms are a concern and noise is an issue, consider using the quiet .17 Remington or a .22 Hornet. Both have mild reports and will cleanly kill coyotes within their effective range if good-quality expanding hollow points are employed.

When to Hunt

Historically, most coyotes have been taken in the fall and winter months. An old trapping rule of thumb stated that any month containing an "R" – September through April – was a good month for fur. Most predator hunters still observe this rule and hunt coyotes from mid-winter (after most other hunting seasons are closed) through spring. Many states allow year-round hunting for coyotes, and I've hunted them in every month of the year in some of these states. While coyote pelts are not prime in the summer, the animals are still challenging to hunt, and the relieved predation on game species and livestock is a valid enough reason in itself to do it.

Regardless of how, where and when you hunt them, coyotes are sure to give you plenty of thrills and challenges. Once you answer the call of the coyote, you will be addicted for life, and there's no turning back. Frankly, I wouldn't care to even if I could.

3

Outfoxing Ol' Foxy

Often regarded as a sport of the English elite, fox hunting dates back to the 16th century. One of the few predators with direct ties to the Old World, foxes are found throughout Europe, parts of Asia and northern Africa.

In the U.S., the two most common fox varieties are the red and the gray. The red fox lives throughout most of North America, from Alaska to Florida and about everywhere in between, with the exception of the extreme Southwest. The gray fox also shares his relative's broad distribution, but has a strong holding in the East, South and some mountain states.

While reds are slightly larger than grays, both are substantially smaller than a coyote or a bobcat. Reds average 8 to 16 pounds; grays weigh 8 to 13 pounds.

Locating Fox Habitat

A few decades ago, foxes were very common in the Midwest and Eastern U.S. Rapid urban encroachment and predation by coyotes have driven them back into niche environments in recent years, however. Not as bold when coming to a call and always extremely wary, foxes offer prime sport as well as beautiful pelts for hunters with the patience to call them in.

Like coyotes, foxes can survive just about anywhere, but without immediately contradicting myself, they're not as adaptable as song dogs and key on more specific habitat. They also have difficulty competing with the larger, tougher coyotes. Traditionally associated with the Midwest and farming country, foxes are still found there in good numbers, although not as many as in former years. I've also hunted them in open prairie country, rocky badlands and even the rain-soaked Pacific Northwest. A secretive, semi-nocturnal animal, the fox is best called in the early morning or late evening, as well as at night.

Fox Guns and Loads

Because foxes are only a quarter to a half as large as a coyote, a cartridge that works well for coyotes can be excessive for foxes. The best cartridge for many fox hunters is one that does little damage to the pelt. In the West, where longer shots are common, the fast-stepping .17 Remington works well, as it generally expends all of its energy inside the animal and does not create an exit wound. The .222 and .223 calibers also are good, but should be loaded with bullets that cause minimal damage. There are two schools of thought on this subject. One is to use a thick-jacketed, expanding bullet (that won't expand with the minimal resistance of a fox) or a completely non-expanding bullet like the Barnes solid or military FMJ. These bullets punch through the fox without causing much damage, and don't provide much shock unless vitals are pierced, so the animal can travel a long way before expiring. The second school of thought is to use a bullet that mushrooms upon impact and expends all of its energy inside the animal. I have found this to be a tricky proposition on small animals. Expecting a bullet to expend a thousand foot-pounds of energy without causing residual damage is my idea of being an optimist. In my opinion, if you're going to shoot any cartridge with energy greater than a .17 Remington, stick with limited- or non-expanding bullets and aim for the heart/lungs.

If you're hunting in a region where shots can be kept within 100 yards, the new .17 HMR will work well, as will the .22 Winchester Mag loaded with rapidly expanding bullets. Either cartridge will anchor a red or gray fox very humanely with correct bullet placement.

Shotguns

In the Midwest, shotguns have been the mainstay of the fox hunter for generations. And they work as well today as they did 50 years ago – in fact, with advance-

Foxes can be found over much of the United States and Europe.

Though foxes can inhabit many different types of terrain, farmland often seems to hold the most animals. In recent years, human encroachment and predation by coyotes have driven foxes back into niche environments.

Fox hunting success: A hard-earned trophy and a great sense of accomplishment.

ments in choke and load technology, they work much better. The type of hunting terrain dictates which choke you should use. Most of the time, a full choke is the best choice. However, it should be noted that a full-choke pattern at distances less than 20 yards does much more damage to the pelt than necessary. If you have a choice, take the shot at 35 yards instead of letting the animal come closer, to minimize pelt damage. While No. 2 shot can be effective on foxes, the smaller shot doesn't always penetrate the animal's thick fur at longer ranges. For this reason, I pick BB or larger, especially when hunting in the middle of winter when the fur is thickest. Also, fewer pellets per payload make fewer holes in the pelt.

Positioning Yourself

Like any type of predator calling, stand selection often is one of the key factors to a caller's success. I prefer a spot that has good visibility, and an easy, unobtrusive approach that has the wind in my favor. I also want a good view of my downwind side as foxes are notorious for circling before committing to a call.

In forests, try to pick an area that allows the hunter to work the edges without physically entering the woods. Creek bottoms, ravines, fence rows and wooded strips all act as natural funnels and help prevent a fox from circling downwind or out of sight. Foxes also tend to follow established trails and escape routes in and out of an area.

Small calibers like the .17 HMR do minimal damage to fox pelts, yet will anchor a red or gray fox humanely within 100 yards with correct bullet placement.

Fox Calls

I have found that foxes seem to be perked more by the high-pitch, squeaky sounds of rodents and birds-in-distress than by jackrabbit or cottontail calls. I like to use small bulb-type squeakers for close-range work, and high-pitched, closed-reed calls for longer setups. I've used electronic calls for all types of predators, but for foxes they're ideal. A large assortment of tapes are available, and many represent birds and rodents. A good feature of electronic calls is that the volume is easily adjusted. When I first get to a setup, I like to call very softly to see if I can interest a fox that's close. If nothing responds, I gradually increase the volume to cover outlying areas. It's been my experience that foxes generally won't travel as far as coyotes when coming to a call.

Accustomed to calling coyotes, the first fox I called was a bit of a surprise and also quite a learning experience. I was calling at one of my favorite coyote hotspots just before dark. After the second calling series, I saw movement 500 yards away at the head of the draw. Looking through my binoculars, I was surprised to see the red fur and a plumed tail bobbing and weaving through the sparse grass and rocks. He was coming on a string to me. At around 250 yards, he disappeared behind a small outcropping of rock. He didn't come out. I could see in every direction around the rockpile, so I knew he still had to be there. After 10 minutes or so of waiting, the light was growing dim and I had only about five more minutes of shooting

Outsmarting ol' foxy is an accomplishment for any hunter.

Shotguns loaded with a stout load of BBs or No. 2s are great medicine for foxes, plus they don't cause too much pelt damage.

light. I decided to sneak to one side where I could see around the rocks and try to spot him. After moving a few yards, I saw him. He was sitting on his haunches, looking around the canyon. He spotted me at about the same time, but luckily with the full camo and the fading light, he paused for just the few seconds that it took to make the shot. It then became obvious to me that coyotes and foxes do not act the same when called. A slow, deliberate, careful approach is more usual for foxes than coyotes. I don't know if they are inherently more call-shy or only fear there may be a larger predator in the area, but the fact remains: It often takes much more patience to call a fox.

If a fox has traveled from a long distance, it often will hang up in the last couple of hundred yards. I don't know if this is to pinpoint the sound or simply to survey the area for signs of danger. When this happens, I switch from a mouth call to a small squeaker bulb. It seems these high-pitched calls interest foxes more and are easier to keep concealed when a fox is inspecting every bush for danger. Because foxes can be apprehensive and shy, sometimes quiet squeaks and whimpers are most effective. Trying to duplicate these noises with a mouth call can be tricky.

The other advantage of an electronic call is that it can be operated remotely. When a fox is poised at 300 yards inspecting the area, it is a lot simpler to turn on a call than to blow one. Also, it's easier to stay undetected if the sound is emitted some distance away from the hunter. This is not possible with a mouth call.

Night Hunting

Where legal, night hunting can be productive for foxes. Like many predators, foxes lose much of their wariness at night and will more readily approach a call. In addition to being less fearful, foxes are very active at night. Taken together, you have a winning combination. I call foxes at night like I do any other predator. Use a red light, set up in an area with good visibility, scan the surrounding area often for eyes, and be ready. Things can happen fast. A shotgun loaded with BBs is the ideal fox medicine under the cover of darkness.

Fox Hunting the Old-Fashioned Way

My father did a lot of fox hunting in his youth in rural Indiana. In the following paragraphs, he explains how they did it back then:

"When the first morning light showed that a fresh snow had fallen, predictable things would start to occur. Telephones would ring a time or two. It didn't take many. Everyone in the neighborhood knew all of the ring patterns on the party line. Anybody who was interested would go "on-line" whether it was for them or not. Morning chores and breakfasts got hurried a little. Shotguns came down from the walls and out from behind kitchen doors. Before long, cars and trucks would start pulling into the driveway. Some belonged to folks who

A secretive, semi-nocturnal animal, foxes respond best to calls early and late in the day, and at night.

Foxes are versatile predators, feeding on everything from small rodents to waterfowl and about everything in between.

didn't even hear the phone. They knew what was going to happen: A fox hunt was aborning!

During the short wait for a straggler or two, coffee was poured and brown paper bags were stuffed with food. We were ready to get it started.

We hunted two ways. Neither was easy or guaranteed, but both worked. I'm sure they still will for foxes, and probably for coyotes. We didn't have any coyotes then, or deer or turkeys. All of them are common now. A fox was the closest thing we had to "big game." There were lots of foxes. There was even a bounty on them. Five bucks! That was a lot of money. It would buy four boxes of shotgun shells at the hardware store.

I'll tell about the easier way first.

It was a "track and ambush" plan. A fresh tracking snow was needed. The area was developed in farming country with county roads on all the section lines, a mile apart in both directions. That was another important part of the hunt.

We could work a hunt with only two or three people, but five was about right. With more than six, it got hard to stay organized and keep track of everyone, so we would split up and do two separate hunts.

We would start by driving around sections of land until we found a fox track going in but not coming out any other side. One hunter would be assigned to follow the track. Before he started, we would drop others on the other three sides at likely crossings to be blockers. Sometimes a

fox would double back on the tracker and come out where he went in, but usually he went on through.

Foxes are creatures of habit. Unless pushed hard or shot at, they will nearly always enter or leave a section at familiar, established places. These crossing are usually at a fence line, a creek bank, an open ditch, a strip of woods or similar obvious feature. They generally avoid open fields and farm buildings. We had hunted the area enough that we knew almost all the likely spots. Three or four blockers could usually cover the crossing points on a section.

We also liked to have a "wheel man" (maybe he'd be called "designated driver" now) to circle the section in a vehicle to keep everyone informed and pick up the blockers for the next stage of the hunt. This was often one of the older fellows who still wanted to take part but didn't like to walk or stand out in the cold anymore.

If we had an extra hunter, he would go with the tracker, staying off to the side for a possible shot and to help keep the fox from doubling back.

Sometimes we would get a fox in the first section, but not always. Foxes are very alert, elusive and unpredictable. They are adept at avoiding an ambush by doing the unexpected. More often than not, one would cross at an unlikely spot, circle the tracker, or simply sneak past a blocker. It was very embarrassing to have the tracker follow a trail right up to your stand and ask, "Why didn't you shoot?"

Occasionally, the fox would not come out at all, but "hole up" somewhere in the section. The area was laced

While foxes are opportunistic feeders and will respond to many different calls, high-pitched rodent and bird calls often produce the best results.

Ambushing foxes while others drive is still a viable method of hunting them.

with buried tile drainage ditches. These came to the surface at a creek, a ravine or an open ditch. If a fox went into one, there was no way to get him out. The hunt was over for him. Or he might climb up inside a hollow tree. Of course, getting a fox was never worth cutting a good den tree. With diligence, a small smoky fire at the bottom might eventually force him to come out. A trip to the nearest junkpile or abandoned fence could yield a length of barbed wire to be fed up the tree, like a Roto-Rooter, and twisted into his fur to drag him out. Usually we only wished him well and looked for another.

If a fox succeeded in getting past us, we would just do the same thing over again on the section he went into. Foxes being what they are, it might take several tries. Some we never did get. They were just too smart or, often, we would start another fox or two during the chase and the original one would slip away. I'm sure we chased a few of the same foxes over and over. They probably enjoyed the game.

A fox wouldn't just light out and leave the area. Around mid-day, the chase would swing around to the right or left. If the fox didn't make a fatal mistake in six or eight sections, by quitting time he'd end up right back where we started. The hunted and the hunters would all be home in time for bed.

The other hunting method was simpler but tougher, and required more hunting skill. It also needed a good tracking snow. Normally two people were involved, although a good hunter could sometimes succeed alone. The approach was simply finding a fresh fox track and following it until someone got a shot. One hunter would stay on the track. The other would work off to the side and make short loops ahead to intercept the fox or push it back into the tracker.

Slow and careful progress is the key to success with this method. It doesn't take long to realize a man can't outrun a fox. If pushed too hard, he will simply run off and leave you behind. Both hunters must move very carefully and keep a close watch for the fox. He will always know that he is being followed but, if not crowded, will at some time make a mistake and allow a shot by a vigilant hunter. It's almost as if he likes the challenge. He may stop and watch his trail to see who's coming. Or backtrack a ways, then take a big hop to one side, just to confuse things. He might even circle the tracker and follow along behind to observe the operation.

We always used shotguns with the first method for everyone's safety, and most shots were at close range. With the second method, shotguns would work, but the extra reach of a rifle was an advantage. Of course, both hunters had to always know where the other would be. Our arsenals were pretty much limited to shotguns and .22s. Rarely, someone would have a .22 Hornet or a .218 Bee for shooting groundhogs. But even a .22 Long Rifle with hollow points would reach a good bit farther than a shotgun.

Foxes will always be considered at the top of the small-predator food chain, due to their natural guile and smart antics.

The second method was a challenge and a lot of fun. But, it almost always meant a *long* hike back to the house or truck at the end of the hunt.

That's how we did it in the old days. Of course, since there's no way to know *exactly* where a fox might go, it's necessary to have advance permission to hunt on a pretty big chunk of land. That wasn't a problem then. Everyone knew everyone else for miles around and permission to hunt foxes was generally granted and understood ahead of time. About half the landowners would be in on the hunt, and most would go at one time or another. Getting permission now may take a little more "neighboring" ahead of time. We all should do a lot more of that anyway."

4

Bobcats and Cougars

Bobcats are more common than most people realize, and can be hunted throughout North America.

Bobcats

While not North America's biggest cat, bobcats make up for what they lack in size with sheer good looks. Numbering around 1 million, these animals are distributed across the U.S. (with the exception of the northern Midwest) and inhabit a wide variety of terrain. In much of their range, thick cover is their chosen home, while in the more open country of the Southwest, they reside in brushy draws, rocky basalt canyons and timbered mesas.

Bobcats are more common than the average hunter realizes, due to their secretive and reclusive nature. Most hunters have the possibility of calling a bobcat within a reasonable drive of their home.

Regardless of where they're hunted, bobcats are a fine trophy and a challenge that should top any predator hunter's list.

Many serious hunters consider bobcats one of the toughest predators to harvest with any consistency.

Bynum on Bobcats

Bill Bynum is a unique individual. When it comes to hunting, he has few equals; when it comes to bobcat hunting, he is the master. Few understand cats like he does. As editor of *Predator Extreme* magazine and *Cabela's Outfitter Journal*, Bynum does a fair amount of hunting, and he also guides bobcat hunters in northwest Tennessee.

The 30-year bobcat hunting veteran says patience is the key to consistently bringing these predators to the gun.

"Unlike coyotes or even foxes, bobcats are slow coming to a call," he says. "They don't bound in looking for an easy meal like a coyote. They slowly sneak in, looking the country over every step of the way. They don't make a move unless they have a pretty good idea of what's going on."

Most predator hunters can't stand this kind of scrutiny, Bynum points out. They either lack patience and don't wait long enough, or they fidget and move too much while calling, ending the game before it ever gets started.

Noted bobcat expert and guide Bill Bynum with a cat whose curiosity got the best of him.

Patience is the key to putting a bobcat in your sights, as these animals are very slow in coming to a call.

Since bobcats don't have a good sense of smell, they use their eyes, Bynum says. "When bobcats come to a call, they have a slow movement that's really hard to detect because they're looking for any sign of danger. Probably over 60 percent of the clients I guide never see a bobcat when it's approaching."

While coyotes are quick to respond to a predator call, usually within 10 to 15 minutes of the initial call, bobcats are much more cautious. Expect to wait at least 45 minutes to spot a bobcat sneaking in to the call, Bynum says. Vigils of over an hour are not uncommon, even in productive areas. "In all of the years I've spent calling them, I've only had one bobcat come in within 10 minutes."

These cats have other idiosyncrasies, too. They prefer to walk dry riverbeds, or soft, moist river-bottom corridors, when approaching a call. Although when making their daily rounds bobcats can cross any type of terrain, they prefer to take the most comfortable approach, due to the soft pads on their feet. If you'll set up and watch the "comfort" corridors, you'll increase your odds of spotting a bobcat.

Tricks of the Trade

An electronic caller and a decoy are a great assistance for tagging a bobcat. Since these animals come in looking for any sign of danger, mouth calling can tip them off to your presence. They can see hand movement, no matter how slight, and locate your exact position by the sound. An electronic caller and a remote speaker will divert the animal's attention away from you.

Bill Bynum says that some calls are much better than others for luring in bobcats. "High-frequency calls seem to work much better for bobcats than anything else I've tried. Bird and rodent sounds far surpass cottontail and jackrabbit-in-distress calls.

"Decoys are another great advantage bobcat hunters have at their disposal," says Bynum. "The decoy does not have to be very sophisticated, either. Over the years I've experimented with a lot of different decoys and have found that a strip of toilet paper or a feather on a piece of fishing line tied to a limb works well. Position the decoy next to the electronic speaker, and you have a winning combination."

Mountain lions are cats to be reckoned with.

Cartridges for Bobcats

Bobcats occasionally grow as large as coyotes, but they generally are smaller and are easier to kill than an average coyote. The largest bobcat I've seen was taken in western Nebraska and weighed 34 pounds. While any coyote caliber will work, those on the lighter end of the spectrum will do a better job of saving the pelt. A .22 Winchester Mag loaded with jacketed hollow-point bullets will work well for close-range work. For longer shooting in more open country, a .17 Remington, .22 Hornet, .222 or .223 is ideal. Shotguns loaded with BB to No. 4 shot also work well in brushy draws and ravines.

Night Hunting

Like all predators, bobcats are active and lose much of their natural fear after sundown. Set up in an area that offers good visibility, such as a short-grass field or a cut agricultural crop with heavy cover nearby. Look for eyes between this cover and the open field. Even at night, bobcats often hang up at the last remaining cover before coming all the way in.

Cougars

Cougars, or mountain lions as they're often called, are North America's largest cat and are on the rise throughout most of their range. While cougar numbers are up, hunting them in many Western states has become more restrictive in recent years. Through public initiative, hound hunting for cats (the most effective means) has been outlawed in several states, and an outright ban on all forms of lion hunting has been in effect in California since 1972. California's lion population has almost doubled to an estimated 6,000 animals in the last 30 years, while their human attack and pet/livestock encounter rate has skyrocketed.

In western Washington, where I'm originally from, hound hunting for cougars was outlawed by public initiative in 1998. Since then, the number of cougars has been on a steady rise from an already stable population. Human encounters with the large cats have also risen dramatically.

While none of our immediate neighbors have been attacked by a mountain lion (although across Washington State, there have been several such cases), most have had livestock, including horses and goats, mauled or killed, even in broad daylight. Every one of them has lost family pets. One morning, my parents' closest neighbor to the south walked out on his porch to get some firewood, and noticed his house cat perched atop the roof of the woodshed. Seeing that the cat was agitated, he softly called to it and reached up for it. It

Using hounds in the snow is a common and highly successful way of finding mountain lions.

jumped over him and hit the ground. Quicker than it takes to tell the story, a mountain lion exploded from the thick underbrush alongside the shed and snatched the cat within feet of its owner. The cougar was a female with two cubs in tow.

By all accounts, cougar populations are on the rise and, with the means of hunting them becoming more and more restricted, hunters need to learn some new tricks to successfully harvest them.

Methods for Hunting Mountain Lions

Spot and Stalk

Let it be known right up front, spotting and stalking mountain lions has one of the lowest success rates in hunting. These cats are spotters and stalkers themselves, and that very nature makes beating them at their own game rather difficult. However, it can be done, and every

Cougars are spry, stealthy animals that can kill elk and with ease.

Hound Hunting

Hunting mountain lions with hounds is the most common and successful method of harvesting these reclusive cats. However, since owning and training a pack of hounds for a single hunt each year is impractical, requiring a lot of time, money and work, most predator hunters hire a full-time hound guide for this type of hunting.

The odds of harvesting a mountain lion are good when hounds are turned loose on the trail. The ingredients for a successful hound hunt are basic: an area with a relatively large population of cougars, a good pack of well-trained hounds, and a hunter with strong enough legs and heart to follow. Once the hounds are trailing a cat, it's the hunter's job to keep up with them.

Hounds can trail mountain lions on dry ground, but the most productive time for trailing is after a light snow or rain. Sign is easier to locate in the rain or snow, and the cat scent clings better to the ground.

Hunting mountain lions with dogs isn't complicated. Hunters drive around known cat haunts until a fresh or "hot" track is located. At this point, the pack is turned loose, and this is when the work begins. Depending upon the age of the track, the cat may have already put many miles between him and you. Even if the track is fresh, the cat is putting some distance between himself and his followers. The dogs will do what they're trained for: follow the track. Some hunters follow the dogs by their bark, trying to keep them in earshot until they hear the "treed bay" and know the dogs have the cat treed. Other hunters use radio collars to keep up with their dogs. Whichever method is used, the chase usually takes the hunters over some rough real estate and hard miles. For those who have not done it, it sounds easy. Those who have done it know it involves a lot of hard hunting and strenuous exercise.

Walking them Up

This technique has become rather popular in Washington State since the outlawing of hound hunting. Done correctly and combined with the right conditions, it can be very productive and will work anywhere cats roam. In fact, it's a great technique for hunters who don't own hounds but still want to "run" a cat. Like hound hunting, hunters cruise around known cat hangouts (either in a truck or snowmobile) after a fresh snow. The best time is after an all-night snow that has stopped sometime before dawn. Any tracks found will be relatively fresh. When the tracks are cut, the hunter starts after them on foot, essentially trying to tree the cat without the aid of dogs. Many times the hunters will spot the cat moving ahead him. I know several hunters who have bagged nice cats using this method, but the problem for most hunters is that you almost have to live in an area with cats and be out at first light after a storm. It's too hard to predict the weather to travel very far in the hopes of a fresh snow.

year a handful hunters fill their tags in this fashion. While it does work, it mainly happens while hunting other species such as elk or deer and it shouldn't be attempted as a sole means of procuring a cougar rug. The odds are simply not in your favor.

Calling

Calling mountain lions is much like calling bobcats, only with a lot less success. This is not because mountain lions won't come to call, but because of their low population density. One male cougar may have a range of over 100 miles! It makes it easy to see that you'll make a lot of stands where a cat won't ever hear you.

However, with diligent calling, cougars can be brought in. It's similar to bobcat hunting in that it takes lots of patience on a stand, minimal movement and a decoy. Stick with fawn bleats and calf bawls since these are a cougar's choice of prey (biologists estimate that a single cougar kills two to three deer a week). The Feather Flex fawn decoy is ideal when used in conjunction with a call.

Photo by Gary Kramer

While hound hunting for cougars has the highest success rate, calling, tracking and even spotting and stalking can work.

Cougar Loads

While mountain lions are strong, muscular predators, they're not as hard to bring down as a bear. Any caliber from .30-30 on up will work fine. Which type of rifle you'll need depends on your style of hunting. For calling and spotting and stalking, an accurate, fast-handling bolt-action rifle such as the Remington Model Seven or Weatherby Super Predator Master with a variable scope is perfect. For hunting behind hounds, a quick-handling, open-sighted rifle such as the venerable Winchester 94 .30-30 is ideal, as shots are close and a rapid second shot may be needed. The bottom line is, no matter which rifle you use, take the time to become familiar with it and be prepared to make an accurate second shot should the situation require it.

5

Black Bears

Ah, yes. Springtime in Alaska. The sun peeked through the dark sky and sparkled the crests of the waves and our breaking wake. In the distance, clouds obscured the snow-covered mountains of Prince of Whales Island. The seat of the open 15-foot skiff pounded my backside as the boat skipped across the chop. Salt spray, rain and occasional sleet stung our faces like bits of gravel. I was trying to stay mounted with a semblance of dignity and act like it was fun. Actually, the second part was easy – I was loving every minute of it.

The engine noise faded and I felt the boat slow down. I turned to face my guide, Brad Saalsaa. Before the boat came to rest, he was on his back across the rear seat, using the starboard gunwale as a headrest while glassing the nearby clearcut. By the time I retrieved my Swarovski ELs from inside my jacket and removed the lens caps, Brad had already spotted a black bear feeding in an open glade. It didn't surprise me. He had been beating me at spotting bears all week

"Where is he?" I asked.

"See that large rock outcropping? Go thirty yards to the left by that old snag."

After scouring this spot for a few minutes, I finally spotted the bear. He popped out of the scenery as if he were alone on a white snow bank. Pinpointing such a large animal out in the open shouldn't be difficult. By the time Brad had given me directions to about 50 different bears, though, I realized that wasn't the case.

"That's a good one," Brad said.

I looked the animal over and had to agree: small ears, long hair, no rub marks, large belly – all the traits of a trophy.

"Let's go for a bit of a hike and see what he looks like up close."

We motored the skiff to the barnacle-encrusted rocks and got out as quietly as possible. I looked up the mountain but could no longer see the bear due to the steep angle and thick underbrush. Close up, the mountain appeared much more daunting than it did from the boat.

We worked our way up the hillside. Slippery blow-downs fooled my feet, and thick brush blocked my view. Soon I was gasping for air from the steep angle and the fast pace Brad had set.

After a good deal of climbing, we crested a ridge and lay down. I had a good view of the bear feeding on some green shoots on a plateau about 250 yards away. We had enough time to look him over from every angle and get a good idea of his size and quality.

I took off my pack and laid it over a short stump. It made a perfect rest. Unslinging my rifle, I flipped up the scope caps and nestled it on top of the soft pack. The Sako .375 H&H with .300-grain Remington Safari loads was sighted to hit 2 1/2 inches high at 100 yards. At 250 yards, I would need to hold roughly 4 1/2 inches high to be on target. The bear was facing me, sitting on its haunches. While I would have much preferred a broadside shoulder shot instead of a frontal shot, I could not be so selective. The brush was thick and if the bear moved, I might not find him again. There was no wind and I had a solid rest, so I decided to risk the shot. Aiming for the white spot on the chest, I squeezed the trigger until the rifle roared to life. When the gun settled from its recoil, I could see the bear lying on his back, all four legs slowly kicking in the air.

Brad slapped me on the back. "Congratulations. That was a great shot!" While we were busy shaking hands and gloating over our success, the bear shook his head and regained his feet.

"Hit him again!" Brad commanded. I shot, and could see the bear stagger. But instead of falling down as expected, he continued walking and even began to pick up his pace. I cycled the bolt and shot again. This time, there was

While not as dangerous as grizzlies, black bears demand a certain degree of respect.

Southeast Alaska is home to some of the world's largest black bears, like this 7-foot, 8-inch trophy.

Bears inhabit a wide range of terrain. When you're spotting and stalking, a bear bedded in a clearcut can still blend in like a rabbit in a brushpile.

not so much as a flinch as the bruin went over a rise and out of sight.

"I'll mark where he disappeared. You go see if you can find him," Brad said.

Because of the rough terrain, reaching the spot where the bear had been was difficult, but in a few minutes I was there. On the ground were splotches of blood and disturbed branches marking his passing. Standing on a tree stump, I looked down into the next ravine and could easily see the blood trail leading into a slash pile as large as a two-car garage.

Glad I used a caliber large enough to leave a good blood trail, I thought. I've seen other bears shot with lesser calibers that hardly bled a drop.

I motioned for Brad to join me. After examining the blood trail, he said, "I'll walk up on that fallen log above the slash pile and try to spot him. You stay here and shoot him if he comes out." I agreed, and off he went.

The top of the slash pile was perhaps 15 feet high. A large alder tree, wet with rain, was lying over the top and a bit off to one side of the pile, and there was a 20-foot straight drop from it to the ground. Clad in knee-high rubber boots, Brad scrambled up the slick log and boldly walked across it, like a trapeze artist on a tightwire. When he was above the slash pile, he paused, peered down into the tangled mess, then turned to me with a grin on his wet face. "You got him! He's lying right here, dead."

But instead of saying "dead," Brad only got out

Author with a Southeast Alaska bear. Much of the hunting in this coastal region is done by boat.

At low tide in coastal areas, black bears can be found walking the shoreline, looking for a meal.

"dea..." when the bear half-roared and grunted below him. Simultaneously, Brad lost his footing on the tree, his arms cartwheeling wildly as he tried to regain his balance.

In my mind, I pictured the consequences of Brad actually falling onto the bear. Realizing that he was not going to recover from the slip, Brad decided to give in to the fall and try to grab the log on the way down. Startled by the commotion above him, the bear shot out of the brushpile. Hanging onto the tree with a demure expression on his face, Brad looked up and quietly said, "Shoot him again." I was more than willing to oblige.

At 20 yards, the slug knocked the bear down, but he instantly regained his feet and sprang for the nearest tree, clawing his way about 10 feet up the rough bark. A final shot through the spine brought the bear out of the tree and ended the excitement.

"Man, what a tough bear!" Brad said, now back on his feet. Still shaken from the experience, I couldn't have agreed more.

On the way back to camp and with the bear stowed securely in the front of the skiff, the word "tough" stuck in my mind. For a single word, it really sums up bear hunting in general. Regardless of how they're hunted, bears always seem to offer more than enough sport for any predator hunter.

I had come to this wettest corner of the continent (a place so wet that hip boots are called "Alaskan Tennis Shoes") to chase the one of North America's largest pred-ators. Grizzly bears, browns and polar bears are, of course, all top predators. However, a hunt for these species requires a guided trip with a large investment in time and money. I choose to hunt black bears because they are more accessible for the average hunter.

Harvesting a black bear can be well within the capability of an independent hunter in many areas. Black bears are more numerous and well-distributed than most people realize. It may be one of our more accessible big-game animals, second only to the whitetail deer.

The historic range of the black bear covered nearly every portion of North America, including all of the lower 48 states. Just as antelope, deer, turkey, coyotes, beavers, eagles, osprey and other species are now common in many areas where they did not exist just a few decades ago, I see no reason that bears cannot re-establish themselves to a large degree. In fact, current populations have reached a nuisance level in some areas, with considerable damage to gardens, orchards, beehives and timberlands.

Black bears, like many animals, adjust surprisingly well to human presence. They are not at all reluctant to venture close to the trappings of mankind. Most residents are not aware of their existence until some obvious damage is discovered. Being mostly nocturnal, silent and very alert, bears are seldom sighted.

We've always had bears around our family home in the Pacific Northwest. My own first bear was taken quite near the house after it had done extensive damage to the orchard and garden. Every year, several bears are killed nearby – all within a few miles of a major population center with millions of people.

Locating Bear Territory

Bears are wary and secretive. They're largely nocturnal, generally non-vocal and can move through even heavy cover as silent as the morning mist. Their broad, padded paws do not leave tracks except in snow or the softest of earth. Therefore, the presence of bears in an area often goes undetected.

The most prevalent evidence of bears results from their foraging – trampled and damaged berry bushes; bent or broken limbs on fruit trees; rotten stumps torn apart for insects; hives of hornets and ground bees destroyed for larvae; bark stripped from living trees for the juicy cambium layer underneath; and probably most important and revealing: feces.

Bear droppings provide valuable insight about the animal's food source and can lead to its whereabouts. Finding the animal's feeding area, be it an alpine berry patch, coastal tideland, fish-spawning stream or abandoned apple orchard, is the key to locating bruins. It's a good bet that a bear will return to a food source daily until the supply is exhausted.

Bears have a "rapid gut." They don't carry their supper very far after a meal. And they're not dainty eaters. The color, texture and content of bear scat can reveal to even the casual observer what food was eaten. Seed, leaves, hair and lumps are often little altered by digestion. Once the food is identified, a search of the local area will often reveal the primary food source.

I've seen droppings packed solid with plum pits. These seeds were over an inch long, rock-hard and sharply pointed on both ends. The mere mental image brings a deeper understanding to the phrase "grumpy as an old bear."

One year, our rather large plot of ripening sweet corn was quickly and totally destroyed. The stalks were flattened as if a pavement roller had been run over them. Oddly, the ears were all missing. There were no stripped and chewed cobs that would indicate activity of raccoons or even deer. Fecal evidence found nearby confirmed that a bear has no patience for such selective and tedious effort. It takes the simple and direct approach: Just chew up and swallow the whole thing, husks, cob and kernels. Let the digestive process sort it out! We did even the score some time later. We ate the bear.

Other signs can show that bears are in the neighborhood. Young cubs are prodigious climbers. Their sharp claws leave distinct scratches on smooth-barked trees like alder, aspen and beech. These marks remain visible for a long time and are solid proof of bear habitation.

Good optics are a necessity for spotting and stalking bears. The country is big and the conditions are generally poor.

Methods for Hunting Bears

I have hunted bears by various means in several states. At certain times, each technique can be exciting in its own right as well as productive. While I certainly have my favorite ways of hunting bears, all of these methods have merit.

Baiting

Baiting is probably the most common method of hanging a tag on a bear. Recently it has come under a lot of criticism and has been restricted or banned in several states. Personally, I don't see anything wrong with baiting bears. It's not my favorite way to hunt, but I have done it enough to know that much skill can be involved. Most hunters who criticize baiting have seen it done in a high-bear-density area with a guide. Baiting in this fashion seems easy because, for the person pulling the trigger, it often is! Where bears are numerous and someone else has been doing the work (scouting and baiting) for several months, coming to sit on a stand for a short time to collect a bear makes baiting seem simple. But turn the tables. Hunt in a lower-density area thick with underbrush, scout out your own spot and haul all of your own bait for a month or two. You will see how much work and skill goes into making a stand a consistent producer. Most will agree that there is more to it than simply throwing a few dough-

Finding fresh bear sign can be easier than you might expect.

There is no finer trophy in North America than a large black bear.

nuts into the woods and waiting for ol' mister blackie to show up.

There are many ways of making a productive bait pile. Here is one I've found to be the most consistent as well as the easiest to prepare. I don't use containers to hold bait. They are unsightly and hard to get into the woods if you have to pack them very far. Instead, I opt to dig a pit roughly 2 feet deep by 3 feet in diameter to put the bait in. I start with cheap commercial dog food covered with corn syrup and anise extract. Put 100 pounds in to start with and cover with several good-sized logs. In a large ring around the site (roughly 6 feet wide), pour a 5-gallon bucket of used cooking oil (that gleaned from restaurant grease traps works great). This serves two functions: First, it adds scent to the area, and second, it gets on the pads of visiting bears, and any other bear that crosses their path is likely to backtrack to locate the source. The addition of grease around a pile can quickly turn a single bear stand into a multiple bear stand.

Check the stand every other day until it's apparent the logs have been moved and bears have found it. Once bears start coming regularly, hang a tree stand and keep adding bait. This is important. Never let the bait run out. If you do, it has been my experience that it will be almost like starting over. I think if bears eat until they are full and must leave food in one spot, they are almost obliged to return until it is gone. If they finish the food, it seems to break this pattern.

Spotting and Stalking

To me, this is the epitome of bear hunting and the method I enjoy most. It can be done almost everywhere the country is open enough and the bear density is reasonably high. Reduced to its essence, spotting and stalking is securing a vantage point, whether that is a boat, a pickup or a high alpine ledge, and using binoculars to scour every square inch of cover until you locate a bear. Then the stalk begins. The most common problem hunters have with spotting and stalking bears is thinking that they've seen all the country has to offer. I realized this mistake while hunting with Brad Saalsaa in Alaska. We would glass a clear-cut as we drifted along with the current. After an hour or so, we would start up the kicker motor and head back to the beginning of the same clear-cut. At first, I wanted to protest. We'd already thoroughly looked over this piece of real estate. But on every pass, we saw new bears. I then realized that if a bear was bedded down, the likelihood of spotting it was extremely low. Only when they stood up and moved around could they be seen – hence the multiple passes.

This technique works no matter where you're hunting. If at first you don't see a bear, but believe it to be a good area, stay put and wait. Chance are, in an hour or so, a bear will get up to stretch his legs.

Calling

During certain times of the year in the right area, calling can not only yield a good bear rug, but also some of your most exciting memories and tales. Like any predator, bears are opportunists, rarely missing an easy meal. As a hunter, this can play to your advantage. A wide variety of predator calls can bring a bruin into range.

However, calling bears is not nearly as easy as calling coyotes, bobcats or foxes, but it's easier than calling cougars. The techniques are the same, but hunters need to mimic a bear's food source to be successful. While a rabbit-in-distress call can sometimes work, to get a bear charged up, the sound has to imitate something large enough to warrant his effort of inspection. A bear is not going to travel a half-mile to eat a mouse, rabbit or small bird unless he is very hungry. But how about a lost fawn or yearling deer? The reward has to match the effort expended, and for bears, this means larger prey.

I prefer to use large, high-volume, raspy, open-reed calls for this type of hunting. Their deeper, throatier sounds carry a long way in dense woods so often frequented by bears and sound convincingly like a fawn or calf elk in distress.

Hound Hunting

Hound hunting, like baiting, has also recently fallen from grace (and legality) in several states. However, where legal, experienced hunters know it's one of the most excit-

Bear sign is often very obvious, like this peeled cedar tree in western Washington. In spring, black bears eat the soft layer of tissue under the bark of evergreen trees.

ing methods of pursuing bears. The hunt is in the chase, not the shot. In fact, the shot is almost anticlimactic. True houndsmen live for the chase alone.

The procedure, in theory, is relatively simple. Hunters usually drive around in pickups on old logging roads until a trail is "struck" by one of their dogs. Once the trail is determined to be reasonably fresh, the dogs are released and allowed to run the trail. Then the excitement begins. Following a pack of excited dogs over mountains and through valleys, over blowdowns and across swamps, is a memorable experience. Bears often take the dogs through some of the roughest terrain imaginable before treeing, and the hunter is obligated to follow. For anyone who says that hound hunting is not sporting, I would suggest that they either haven't done it or had an extraordinarily uneventful chase.

Targeting Natural Food Sources

If you can't bait where you live, or don't want to go through the hassle, mess and work of it, there is another way of predictably harvesting bears over "bait" that is easy and universally legal: It is targeting natural food sources. During the early spring and early fall, bears are almost obsessed with eating. Most of their waking time is spent finding food. Hunters can use this to their advantage if they can find where the bears are dining. In the early spring, bears' stomachs are still delicate from a winter of non-use. Carrion does not hold the appeal in the spring as it does in the fall. Instead, bears prefer a diet consisting largely of grass, skunk cabbage and, around coastal areas, mussels, crabs and barnacles.

As summer progresses, berries become a larger part of their diet. To a bear, almost anything is food, from suburban sweet corn patches to fruit or even garbage. In wilderness areas, look in the high country. Berries of different varieties are getting ripe by summer, and to a bear, this is one huge bait pile. Look for stripped berry branches, bear scat and worn trails with fresh tracks. Once a bear is using

Bear hunting is often an adventure of the highest order. Prepare for the worst in weather and expect to get wet.

Scent Control

This may be the most often overlooked aspect of bear hunting and has unfortunately caused many a hunter to miss an opportunity. Like all animals, bears have their strong and weak points. To be honest, they are as myopic as a bat. Their hearing is reasonable, but not stellar. But their nose is out of this world. They may have the best sense of smell of any predator.

I have known this and have seen it displayed often over the years, but recently in Alaska I saw it occur again, and it still amazes me. A partner and I were cruising around in a skiff looking for bears on the beaches at low-tide mark. Soon we saw one, slowly working his way down the beach toward us, rolling rocks over to get at small crabs. We cut the engine and watched him through the binoculars. He was a nice 6-foot-plus bear with no rubs, but because much larger bears were available, he was not a shooter. The wind was blowing almost parallel along the stretch of coastline from him to us. The skiff, drifting from tide and remnants of its own motion, inched closer to the shore until I heard the muted crunch of barnacles under the bow. Now essentially resting on the shoreline, we sat still as the bear ambled closer. From 100 yards to 75 and then 50, he continued towards us. I figured that even with poor eyesight, he would surely spot us at any second. I mean, here were two guys sitting upright in a shiny aluminum boat less than 50 yards away, but continue closer he did. At less than 25 yards away, we could hear the bear's claws scraping the barnacle-encrusted rocks. I sat stock-still, and even when the bear looked right at us, he did not recognize us. Now he was less than 10 yards away and still continuing along the same course. With each step he grew closer until he was literally right in front of the boat, only feet away. If I had a fishing rod, I could have swatted him on the butt. He took another step, rolled over another rock and then relieved himself within 3 feet of the bow of the boat (which goes to prove that bears don't always "go" in the woods). Now with his back toward us, he continued down the beach in his search for more protein. About 100 yards away, the shoreline swept outward on a little point. The bear, following the natural curvature of the land, was soon at a point directly downwind from us. With the first slight breeze, he stopped walking, lifted his nose to the air and immediately turned tail and headed right back the way he had come. While he thought he was fleeing from danger, he actually again crossed our bow within a few feet and continued back into the safety of the evergreen forest. Two points about bears were heavily reinforced. They can't see worth a hoot, but their noses are pretty darn good!

There are a couple of ways a hunter can overcome this keen sense. Several years ago, I started using scent-eliminating wash for my clothes, scent-free shampoo,

an area, it's likely that he will continue to do so. The berries will keep ripening at increasing elevations throughout summer and fall. Often, the active berry bear will follow this ripe line uphill until frost and the berries are gone.

Growing up in Washington, I quickly learned that not only people treasure a sweet apple; bears do as well. Scattered across the countryside are many abandoned apple orchards, overgrown with brush but still producing heavy loads of apples. As the crop ripened, bears would move in, first cleaning up the fallen apples then climbing the tree to get the remaining ones. It was easy to determine when a bear was using a particular patch. The tree trunks showed claw marks, and limbs were broken and hanging.

Not far away were dung piles full of apple seeds and residue. Simply sitting near an apple tree and waiting will often provide an opportunity for a shot. If a bear is going to show, it often will be at last light, so good light-gathering optics are useful for this type of hunting.

As Robert Ruark said, "Use enough gun." This definitely applies to bear hunters.

soap and deodorant, and then covered up with natural wood cover scent. This technique worked OK, but only for a short time. One hot afternoon in a stand was all it took to ruin any scent elimination I had. More recently, I have been using activated charcoal suits, and have found them incredibly efficient in eliminating odor. Best of all, they can be thrown in the dryer and easily recharged for the next hunt.

In addition to doing everything possible to eliminate scent, using air currents to your advantage is extremely important. When stalking, approach from downwind. If calling, sit in a spot where the logical path for the bear is upwind from you. If you are baiting, hang a tree stand high enough so your scent is carried far away in the breeze. Have more than one stand site pre-selected to accommodate any wind direction.

Shooting Bears

I recently read in a national outdoor magazine a question from a reader about suitable guns for bear hunting. The responder made the statement that a bear would not go very far after being hit in a vital spot with any good deer caliber in the .270, .30-06 or .308 class. I can't disagree with this statement. Any hunter with such a caliber who encounters a bear should be able to take it, provided he can shoot well. There are, however, other factors that must be considered when hunting bears, especially in certain types of habitat.

Bears are not as susceptible to shock as higher-strung animals such as deer, antelope and even elk. Bears have a disturbing habit of "dropping dead" in their tracks when shot and then, like a rubber ball, bounce to their feet and scoot out of sight into the nearest bushes.

"Not very far" is a relative term when it involves cover like the coastal rain forest of Alaska and the Pacific Northwest. The vegetation is so heavy that it's hard for strangers to comprehend. The underbrush is much higher than a hunter's head and so dense, he often can't see his own feet. A full-sized bear, dead or alive, is hidden at 10 feet. Bears often don't leave a good blood trail because of the heavy fur and fat layer under the hide. It's usually very wet or raining, especially during spring hunts, which disperses blood spoor quickly. Rather than the standard waiting period, an immediate follow-up is called for, maybe on hands and knees.

Keep in mind that at this stage of the game there is no way to tell if the bear in question is dead, dying or only severely annoyed.

Robert Ruark said, "Use enough gun." I concur with that for bears. Use the biggest gun that you can shoot well. Remember, no further action is committed until you take the first shot. Make it a good one. Take your time and be positive you can hit a vital spot. If the bear drops dead, shoot it again right away to be sure. If it starts running, hit it again and as often as you can as long as it's in sight.

6
Scent Control

A coyote's nose is his first line of defense — fool that, and you often fool the dog.

The coyote was bounding directly toward our position. The wind was perfect, blowing lightly from the dog to us. When he cleared the top of the ridge in front of us, roughly 300 yards away, he paused to survey his surroundings.

Suspicious. Cautious. He may have played this game before.

Embarking again on his journey, he left his old track at right angles to where we'd been calling. Down the valley he went. It was clear he was going to try to circle our calling stand to let his nose confirm what his ears had heard.

Before I could change positions and ready myself for a shot, the coyote disappeared around the corner of the valley. I lay there and waited. In less than three minutes I heard the single, flat echo of a shot across the open landscape. I listened eagerly. No more shots followed. I thought to myself, *That's a good sign. One shot usually means a dead dog, two means maybe a dead dog and three means a definite miss.*

I stood up and walked around the small knob to where my partner Taro Sakita had been perched. He was already standing up and slinging his rifle, getting ready to walk the 200 yards to the fallen coyote.

He spoke what I guessed. "I let him get as close as he could, but if he had angled any more, he would have smelled us."

Knowing the wind direction is critical when predator hunting. There are several products available that help, but the time-proven method of sifting dust still works.

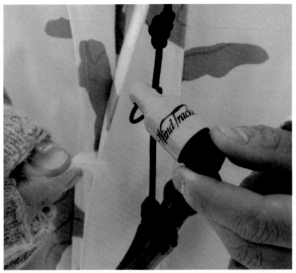

Wind indicators work even when the wind is really light. They also show subtle currents that are hard to detect with other methods.

Taro was right.

I've seen coyotes as well as other predators circle callers so many times, it's something I now plan for. It wasn't by accident that Taro was sitting on the opposite side of the hill, covering the back door. The fact of the matter is, he's a better shot than I am, and by the time a coyote circles the backside of a calling station, it usually is either running flat out or a long way off. So I had placed Taro accordingly.

Coyotes, foxes and bears have a phenomenal sense of smell. Deer have around 10 million scent receptors inside their nose compared to our paltry 10,000. I've never taken the time to count a coyote's scent receptors, but I've seen them smell things a deer would never notice – and at much longer distances. Coyotes can smell on par with deer, and quite possibly even better. Bears have about everything beat by a country mile. Their sense of smell is downright spooky.

Since predators are so wary and have such a keen sense of smell, a novice hunter may wonder how anyone is able to bag them with any consistency. The answer is not simple, but it reinforces why we choose to hunt predators in the first place: If predator hunting were easy, it would be reduced to simply killing and would have no appeal.

Scent Avoidance

The best way to beat a predator's sense of smell is to simply avoid it in the first place. Staying downwind of the animal, hunting with the wind in your face, is much more effective than relying on scent-elimination products, cover scents or scent-absorbing clothing.

Defeating a predator's nose starts with choosing the right setup, which forces an upwind approach. Look for canyons where the only good advance is up a

single draw, or at the head of a canyon where a bare field is at your back. Anything that helps funnel the predator's movements toward you is a benefit and should be utilized.

Try as you might, however, there will be times that you'll be forced to set up in a less-than-ideal spot because of terrain. In fact, when the wind is blowing hard, I often call directly downwind, as it is the only direction sound will carry any significant distance. While this is the worst case for having a predator smell you, it may be the only chance one will be able to hear your call in the first place. Granted, this is not ideal, but when given the choice between ignoring the wind or simply going home, I take it. Calling under the worst conditions will always provide more coyotes and more sport than sitting in the living room watching TV!

Detecting the Wind

Detecting wind direction seems simple, right? In a strong gale it is, but when the wind is gusting or just slightly moving with the thermals, it is a lot harder than those old Indians in the B-grade Western movies made it look. While dropping sand from your fingers can work, there are better ways to detect the wind. Over the last few years, I have been using two products that work extremely well. The first is called "Smoke in a Bottle." Essentially, it is an extremely light powder in a squeeze bottle. Flip the top open, squeeze the bottle and voila! – a stream of white "smoke" erupts, drifting in the air currents. Detecting wind direction, even in the slightest breeze, has never been easier and one bottle will last for many hunting seasons.

The second product, called the Wind Tracker from Cabela's, is an adaptation of the same idea, only it is a small container that attaches to a D-ring or a zipper on your jacket and contains lightweight fibers similar to goose down. Simply pull a piece from the container (the next one pops out ready for use, much like a tissue dispenser), and let it drift in the wind. The nice thing about this product is that, as it drifts with the wind, you can see it for a long distance to alert you of any swirls or eddies away from you. The fibers will also hold your favorite scent.

Adapting

What should you do when conditions are less than ideal? It's common for a coyote to approach from the downwind side, where it can easily pick up on your scent. Also, coyotes frequently circle a caller, trying to approach from the downwind side. For these situations, you need to have a partner covering the back door. Or, you can set up

Robinson Labs makes some excellent scent-elimination products, from shampoo to laundry detergent to deodorant.

If the wind is shifting and unpredictable, spray down with scent eliminator before every set.

in a position that allows easy movement and a view of all directions. This is tough to accomplish and not always practical. A second hunter is usually a better way to go.

I typically try to call from a slight ridge or promontory where I have good visibility of a wide range. By placing the second hunter 180 degrees in the rear looking downwind, you both have good visibility and a 360-degree angle of coverage. The downwind shooter needs to be fully aware of the wind angle and be prepared to shoot, even if the animal is not as close as he would like. It doesn't take long for a spooked predator to head for the hills, presenting no shot opportunity at all. Obviously, when using such a site, try to stay hidden in some cover below the crest to avoid silhouetting yourself against the skyline.

Although I rely on "Adapting" and "Avoidance" to get around a predator's keen sense of smell, there are also many commercially made products that can increase your odds of success. I use them in conjunction with each other for those times when things don't go quite as planned.

No Scent Makes Sense

Eliminating scent starts at the body level. I don't believe cover scents or scent-eliminating products are effective if a hunter isn't clean to begin with. Many animals can smell at least 100 times as good as a human. They also have the ability to distinguish between multiple scents simultaneously. That means they can smell rabbit urine,

some sage scent and, oh, yes, a little bit of rank human, all at once.

For this reason, I start out by using scent-eliminating shampoo and body soap in the morning shower, followed by scent-free deodorant. I also wash my clothes in a scent-eliminating wash, and air dry them outside where they won't likely absorb any human- or man-made scents (automobile exhaust, cooking fumes or campfires). I then keep the clothes stored in a sealed bag with a couple of cuttings of sage until I go hunting.

Masking Human Scent

Once afield, I generally don't use cover scents but instead rely on one of the commercial scent-eliminator sprays available. I spray down my face, hair, hat, clothes boots and gear with it. These products really work, but they need to be applied liberally and often, especially in hot weather.

Even though I don't use cover scents, I know many hunters who do and swear by them. Many varieties of cover scents are available, ranging from dirt to sage to rabbit urine and everything in between

That all done, you can go afield and hunt. Seem like a lot of work? It is. That's why I was so excited when new technology in the form of carbon-activated clothing hit the scene a few years ago.

Out on the open plains, wind currents can be fickle and hard to predict from one stand to the next. But by paying attention and using scent-eliminating products, you can still be successful.

Activated carbon clothing is the best option for hunters who are serious about fooling a predator's nose.

Activated Carbon Clothing

When activated carbon clothing was introduced, it was in the form of a liner suit designed to be worn under a set of camouflage hunting clothes. While it worked, it was extremely hot to wear. For whitetail hunters perched in a tree stand in cold weather, it was fine. For mobile hunters in areas where daytime temperatures rise into the 70s, it was out of the question.

Since those early liners became available, a lot has changed in the activated carbon market. Today's carbon clothing is a lot more effective at containing odors. These products have also become lighter. Finally, they are now being made right into many garments with very little additional weight or bulk.

Activated carbon absorbs more scent than any other material, which is why it is so often used as an air/water filter. It is relatively expensive, and it doesn't really wear out or "fill up." It is easy to recharge back to its original state by simply throwing it in a standard clothes dryer for 30 minutes on high.

Once activated, carbon clothing can be worn for several days to a week before it needs to be recharged. I store mine in a scentproof bag, where it remains effective until it's used.

I have tried Robinson Labs', Scent Blocker, Cabela's Scent Pro and GORE-TEX Supprecent activated carbon clothing, all with good success. The first two contain about an equal amount of scent-absorbing material, but for lightweight wear in warm weather, it is hard to beat the GORE-TEX Supprecent.

Recently, I have been wearing the new 3D light jacket and pants from Robinson Labs and find them perfect for most predator hunting applications. The 3D material is the finest available, giving a great profile and blotchy appearance, and the scent-absorbing abilities are unsurpassed for its weight.

Regardless of which road you take to scent elimination, be sure to always remember that a predator's nose is one of its first lines of defense and should not be ignored. That means avoidance, adaptation and preparation.

7
Making a Stand

Frequently the difference between bagging a predator and going home empty-handed is choosing the right calling spot. I personally feel this is more important than actual calling technique, scent control and camouflage combined. Select the right stand, and over half the battle is already won. Pick the wrong spot, and no amount of good calling will make it productive.

Back when I was first learning to hunt predators, selecting a stand was the first real difficulty I encountered. I already knew how to call. I had my rifle sighted in properly. But time after time I'd get skunked and didn't know why. Typically, I would just walk out into the desert, plop down when I felt I walked far enough, and start calling. After an hour or so of not seeing a coyote, I'd walk some more and repeat the process. I almost always went home with an empty bag, except for the occasional unlucky coyote I jumped while walking.

If it hadn't been for dumb luck, I might have become so frustrated with predator calling, I would have given it up entirely. One thing I did right was pay attention to what worked, then tried to emulate it in the future.

One day while predator hunting (others may have called it aimlessly stumbling through the country), I topped a rise. The light 5 mph breeze was blowing directly in my face. The only reason I noticed it was because of the putrefying odor. A dead cow or some other rotting animal was somewhere in the distance. Before I could investigate the source of the smell (exactly what any 13-year-old would want to do), I looked out across the small valley and saw a coyote mousing in a small grass patch. He was perhaps 500 yards away and had not seen me top the small ridge. (I hadn't even thought about slowly poking over the hill, glassing as I went.) I quickly sat down and nestled in among some small sage bushes. I shouldered my rifle and located the coyote through the scope. I settled the crosshairs on the speck of coyote. Before I impa-

tiently pulled the trigger, I talked myself down, knowing the odds of making the shot were about one in a million. I kept my rifle across my knee and raised a call from the lanyard that hung around my neck.

The first breath of air through the old Circe whipped the coyote's head around. The second burst brought him on a dead run. He ran in a straight line towards me. For the first couple of hundred yards, he came on like an Olympic sprinter. Then he turned at a right angle towards me and began to skirt the diminutive hill I was sitting on, trying to get downwind (I know this now, but not then). He angled as far to my right as he could go, but the lay of the land prevented him from getting directly downwind of me. He continued towards me, now at a trot instead of a run, pausing every so often to look over his shoulder. A quiet squeak through the call kept him coming. When he closed to 100 yards, he paused, trying to zero in on the sound before coming closer. I centered the crosshairs and took the shot. He folded like a cheap lawn chair. Dragging him back to camp, I reflected on the situation and asked myself, *Why did this coyote respond to my call and not others on previous hunts?* Obviously, my calling sounded good enough. Then I remembered his circling. How many other coyotes had come in and, because of my position, I never saw them?

As the years progressed, I became more aware of the importance of setting up in the proper location. Each passing experience confirmed these beliefs. Now, after 15 years of heavily hunting coyotes, I can look at an area, pick out a spot to call from and have a pretty good idea of what my chances are of seeing a coyote. If the country is good and the stand is good, the odds are pretty high that I'll spot one, but if the country is good and the stand is poor, I know not to expect much. Most hunters who have chased coyotes a lot can also do this. Why? Because picking a prime calling location is relatively constant from area to area.

Knowing what to look for when choosing a calling spot is vital to predator hunting success.

Corridors like his one, when combined with the right cover, provide some fast-paced coyote shooting.

What Makes a Good Stand?

The first thing you want to look for in a calling area is an elevated position. This doesn't have to be a mountain or an extremely large hill, just high enough to provide good visibility over any underlying cover or depressions in the land. While this is a big part of choosing a stand, it's also area-specific. In sagebrush that's waist- to chest high, it's absolutely necessary. In a river bottom, evergreen forest or open wheat field, calling from an elevated stand may not be as important, but it's still preferable.

Accessibility to a calling area is also important. I like to be able to slip into an area without being seen. This is another reason a small rise works well. You can walk in behind it, using it for cover, then slowly sneak over and get into position. This is where wind plays a role. The wind needs to be moving from the calling area to the stand.

I prefer large calling areas over small ones. All of the other important features – a small rise, a slight wind, offering a concealed approach – can be there, but if the area is small, chances of a coyote hearing and responding to your calls are reduced. While a large area usually means coyotes are more apt to be present, don't overlook small honey holes simply because the calling area is not large. Brush rows, old abandoned homesteads and small patches of cover all can make excellent coyote habitat.

Sneaking In

As mentioned in the last section, sneaking in to a calling area is of vital importance. While it's essential that a predator not spot your approach, it's also equally important that it doesn't smell or hear you.

Just recently, I took a friend coyote hunting. He told me on the drive out that he had hunted coyotes several times, but except for the occasional "jumped" coyote, he'd never shot one responding to a call. We got to the area and I parked the pickup. The area was just off a dirt road, less than 200 yards away, but the truck was screened from view and I had great success there on previous trips. We got out of the vehicle and I quietly closed the door behind me, not even closing it all the way for fear of making too much noise. Not thinking I needed to warn him, he got out of the truck and slammed his door with a resounding noise. I looked over at him with a scowl, but he wasn't paying attention. He apparently thought nothing of it! I didn't like the noise the door made, but since we were already there, I figured it couldn't hurt to go ahead call anyway. My partner came around the truck and asked in loud voice, almost a shout, "You think there are any coyotes here?" I thought to myself, *Some coyotes probably were here, but not now.* No wonder he'd never called in a coyote.

Predators have excellent hearing. That is why a call works so well. Think about it. If a coyote is capable of hearing a rabbit-in-distress call over a mile away, he

When picking a calling location, try to find some cover to break up your outline. Even in open country, there's almost always some vegetation or terrain feature to hide in.

An elevated calling position makes spotting incoming predators much easier.

Areas like this one — lots of broken country with plenty of places where a predator might hide — make for great calling zones.

won't have any problem picking up a human-made noise such as a truck door slamming or loud talking at half that distance.

The hunt starts when you kill the vehicle's engine. Everything you do from that moment forward affects your success. This means not only do you have to get to your calling stand unseen, but unheard as well.

Also, if approaching the stand is going to spread your scent into the calling area, it's best not to call from that spot (there are exceptions to this rule as described in Chapter 8). It only takes a few times of associating a sound such as a rabbit call with a human scent, and the game is up. Odds are, you will have an extremely hard time calling that same coyote for quite awhile.

Locating Howls

When I approach a calling location I'm not familiar with, I often use a single lonesome howl to locate a coyote's position before setting up. I find this technique works well, and I believe it also doubles as a territorial call for those animals defending their area.

Once You're There

Once you find and successfully get to an ideal calling stand, what next? I am sure everyone has their own tried-and-true routine, but here's what works for me. Before I do

anything, I thoroughly scan of the calling area with binoculars. It's amazing how many times you'll spot a coyote before blowing the first note. Once I've satisfied no coyote is visible, I take my binoculars off and lay them next to me, within easy reach. I don't like anything bulky like binoculars hanging around my neck. They get in the way while shouldering a rifle or can clang against the rifle stock, spooking any predator that's close. I put on my face mask and gloves, and I lay out any calls that aren't on the lanyard around my neck -- generally my howler and squeaker calls.

I start off with a close-range rabbit-in-distress call or a squeaker in case a coyote is within a couple hundred yards. After I do a series of calls (roughly 30 seconds), I pick up my binoculars and rescan the area. After several minutes of waiting and looking, I use a long-range, open-reed caller such as the All-Call and do a loud series of cottontail-in-distress calls for about 30 seconds. Next, I re-scan the area with binoculars, this time for upwards of five minutes. If nothing has shown up by this time, I repeat the previous calling sequence. If a coyote shows up, watch his body language. If he's approaching your stand without any encouragement, let him come and keep silent. If he stops, looks around or hesitates like he needs some more incentive to approach, give it to him. Call very quietly until you can tell he's heard you. If this doesn't convince him to come closer, get more "needy" with the call – not necessarily louder, but just more pitiful and injured.

Picking a spot correctly often leads to a heavy but rewarding pack out.

In extremely open country, it's not always possible to blend in with the surroundings. But you can keep below the horizon and keep your movements to a minimum.

Should I Stay or Should I Go?

There comes a point during every stand when you're pressed with the question, "Should I stay or should I go?" There is no hard-and-fast rule, and only you can make the decision. Each stand is different. When I'm calling coyotes, I generally only stay at one location for 15 to 20 minutes. However, there are times when I break this rule. If I'm hunting in a small pocket of brush where I know a coyote is only going to be several hundred yards away, I may only stay 10 minutes and try to cram as many of these short stands into a day as possible. On the other hand, if I'm in an area where I know a coyote is present, either through visual or audible confirmation, I stay much longer.

I once had a coyote sit on a ridge several hundred yards away and just stare in my direction. The wind was right, and he'd not seen me, but he just wasn't convinced by my calling. In such a situation, I keep calling until the animal either goes away or decides to come in. The last stand of the evening is also an exception to my 15-minute rule. Often I get into position 30 minutes or so before sundown, and start calling. By the time I've completed the normal 15-minute time frame, it's too late to leave and find another stand location before dark, so it's often best just to keep calling until there is no shooting light left. Occasionally, a late-coming dog will respond right before dark.

Tight Stands

Every hunter gets in the habit of sticking with what works. There is nothing wrong with this, for if it worked once, it's bound to work again. But there are times when a radical change-up is needed. Most of us like to set up in areas that offer great visibility of a lot of open country, but don't overlook those brush-choked river bottoms and woodlots. Coyotes, as well as other predators, often call them home

Recently, while hunting with Trophy Mountain Outfitters in southern Colorado, I had my own time-tested techniques challenged a bit and learned something in the process. We'd been calling coyotes in typical open coyote country choked with small juniper trees and riddled with rocky canyons. It was ideal calling territory, and we were doing very well. Like much of southern Colorado, the landscape changed drastically, and by first light the following morning, I found myself with guide Dean Silva, set up in a thick river bottom. The grass was waist-high, with tons of underbrush and trees to obscure my view of the area. Even though I wouldn't have picked this location by myself, I thought, *Oh well, when in Rome* … and started calling. Five minutes later, a coyote literally exploded from the long grass and stood in a small clearing 20 yards away. A shot from my partner's .243 got him spinning, and Dean finished him off with his .257 Ackley Improved. I was shocked. It was no surprise that there was a coyote in the river bottom. The country looked good

Shade and objects that break up the human outline make it much more difficult for a predator to spot you.

enough and I had called coyotes out of tight cover before, but I had never actually set up smack dab in the middle of it. I've always been in the habit of setting up on the outside of heavy cover or, even when in the thick of it, looking for a spot that yielded at least 50 yards of open terrain around my position. I had passed up many good-looking spots over the years simply because I couldn't find a calling stand that met all of my requirements. Not anymore. If the country is tight and the brush is thick, set up anyway. Get a large tree or brushpile behind you, and start calling. The odds still can be pretty good that a coyote will be in your lap before you can say "boo."

8

Calls and Calling

Whether you use electronic or mouth calls, the thrill of watching a coyote run to a stand is still the same.

When I first started hunting coyotes, I would simply walk along the pastures and cropfields of our rural area, hoping to catch a glimpse of these sly predators. Occasionally I was successful, but if coyotes were meals, I soon would have starved.

I had heard about calling and had even gone so far as to buy a Murray Burnham video. I was amazed at what I saw. Coyotes by the dozens came running like chickens at feed time whenever the old pied piper of predators sounded off on one of his flutes. Of course, I hurriedly rushed out and spent my hard-earned lawn mowing money on a call.

Like many tyro predator hunters, I was more than a bit disappointed when I spent a full day afield calling, just like ol' Murray did on the video, and not getting as much as a glimpse of a coyote.

Looking back, it's easy to see why I failed. To begin with, I didn't pick my calling stands with any forethought. I just plopped down wherever the fancy struck me. It didn't matter if I could see five yards or 500. Moreover, I didn't pay any attention to the wind, ignoring the coyote's incredible sense of smell. And I made the most common mistake of novice callers – staying too long in one place. I would often sit in one location for an hour or more, then walk only several hundred yards to the next ridge to try again. Today, I rarely sit longer than 15 minutes in one spot, and only then if I've heard a coyote howl or have seen signs of their presence.

When I was just about ready to hang up calling and go back to being an opportunistic predator hunter, it all came together. I was hunting around the L.T. Murry Game Range in eastern Washington and came upon a large valley. The wind was in my face, though I didn't pay much attention to wind direction at the time. I sat down next to a gnarled old stump, laid my rifle across my lap, and began to call. After the first series of short calls, I picked up my binoculars to glass the surrounding area. The entire field of view was a close-up of moving, shifting gray fur! Pulling the binoculars away from my face, I saw a coyote less than 50 yards in front of me, running madly in my direction. Shouldering the rifle, I jerked off a shot. The bullet flew past the kamikaze coyote and crashed into the rock canyon behind him. Confused by the noise, he stopped to look around. With as much coordination as my pounding heart would allow, I cycled the bolt. Taking a deep breath, this time I squeezed the trigger. The coyote collapsed where he stood. I was hooked and finally knew first-hand that calling would work.

I've talked with many novice callers over the years, all looking for advice or "tricks" to make it easier. While I can't say there are many tricks to being a successful caller, there are a few fundamental techniques that, with regular practice, will help bring success.

The first rule is to call where the animals are. One season, I recorded my calling success rate at stands where I knew a coyote was in the area (either through visual sightings or by howling) as compared to blind calling (just going into an likely looking area and setting up). When I knew a coyote was in an area, I could bring it within shooting range 90 percent of the time. For the blind stands, the rate was only around 20 percent. It's easy to see where the best odds are.

This is not to discourage anyone from blind calling. In fact, it's almost impossible to hunt predators without doing a lot of blind calling in new areas. It would be nice if I could know a coyote was in every area before I called, but this is simply not possible. The key to success is covering a lot of terrain. I try to adopt the motto of door-to-door salesmen: every rejection is just one step closer to a sale. The same is true for predator hunters. You have to knock on a lot of doors and get rejected before someone decides to buy your line.

I found another interesting trend in my collected data. Of all the coyotes I called, 65 percent came within the first five minutes. Thirty percent came between five and 15 minutes, and only 5 percent came after 15 minutes. Depending upon the region, population density and time of year, results may differ, but my discussions with other callers indicate they won't differ much.

Electronic calls can play a big part in your hunting strategy.

Taken together, these numbers show an obvious trend: Success for blind calling is low. Therefore, the more stands you can squeeze into a day, the better your chances of closing a deal. The success rate is high if a coyote is in an area. Locating a coyote by sight, sound or responses to a howler is very important. Coyotes respond quickly to a call. Don't stay in one place too long. I feel the best combination is to stay only about 15 minutes and then hustle to the next spot. If you wait for 30 minutes, you will occasionally pick up a slow-responding coyote, but you will only make half as many stands during the day. The overall odds of getting a shot will be less.

Selecting a Call

Successfully calling predators is part hunting skill, part experience, part proper technique and part choosing the right call and using it correctly. The first parts of the equation come with time and exposure, but the final part, choosing the right call, is easy. Here is a breakdown of the major calls available.

Mouth calls are loud enough to carry long distances on relatively calm days.

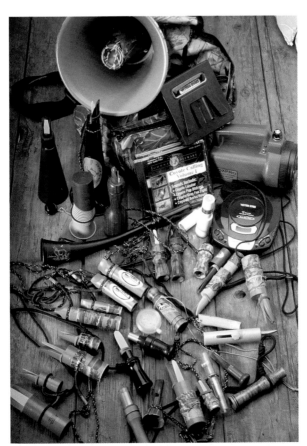

Calls come in every shape in size, from the extremely high tech to the very basic.

Mouth Calls

Over the years, I've probably used 30 different models of mouth calls. While they all worked well, there are times when different styles are more desirable than others. In today's high-tech society, the uninitiated may think mouth calls are on their way out; being replaced by more sophisticated mechanical and electronic calls. Nothing is further from the truth. At last count, there are over a dozen main manufacturers of over 50 different mouth calls for predators, and more than a 100 custom-call manufacturers. And why not? Mouth calls still hold a significant niche and are an advantage to serious predator hunters.

First, they're cheap. A hunter can buy a mouth call for about 5 percent of what an electronic call costs. They're also easy to carry in a pocket, as they weigh virtually nothing. They work well, too. I've taken mouth calls all over the U.S. and into several African countries, and without exception have had predators come running to the sounds these calls made.

Mouth calls are also durable and dependable. My first call was a simple Burnham mouth call. After 15 years of predator calling, I still have this call and it still brings in plenty of coyotes. There are many other options for callers today that weren't around even a few years ago, but mouth calls are still the predator hunter's standby. They're not all the same and can be broken into three types: closed reed, open reed and howlers. Bulb calls are not technically a mouth call, but share the same advantages and are used in a similar way.

Mouth calls are cheap, versatile and easy to carry afield.

Closed-Reed Calls

My old Burnham call is a closed-reed call, as are many of the manufactured calls on the market today. Essentially, a closed-reed call is a straight tube (either plastic or wood) with a fixed reed inside that vibrates as air is forced past it. These calls can produce a variety of sounds with different air volume, hand control and voice manipulation. The big advantage of closed-reed calls for the novice is that they're easy to use: simply cup with one hand, and blow. That's it. Growling into the call will produce a lower, raspier sound, larger volumes of air create a higher-pitched wail, and short bursts create the sounds of a small rodent. Some closed-reed calls come with different reed sizes that can imitate different species (from fawns to mice) or increase or decrease the distance the sound carries.

One of my favorite calls is the Lohman with three enclosed reeds for short, medium or long range. It's handy to have a single call that's so versatile around your neck. Another closed-reed favorite is the Primos Raspy Coaxer. This call has a medium reed in place for general work, but it also has a small squeaker reed that can be used for up-close convincing.

The disadvantage of closed-reed calls is that they tend to freeze up in cold weather. Moisture gets in between the reed and the tube, and freezes. Some of these calls are better than others, but at one time or another, I've had all my closed-reed calls freeze up and often at precisely the wrong time. If you're hunting in below-freezing weather,

Closed-reed calls are simple to use and easy to learn, but do not offer the versatility of an open-reed call.

the best technique is to place the calls inside your shirt pocket underneath your hunting parka, where they will stay warm. Letting them dangle around your neck in cold weather is asking for problems.

Open-reed calls sound great and don't freeze up in cold weather, but they take a bit more practice to master than other types of mouth calls.

Open-Reed Calls

Over the past few years, I've grown quite fond of open-reed calls. I initially avoided them, as they're somewhat harder to learn to use than closed-reed calls. An open-reed call still utilizes an outside tube of wood or plastic, but instead of having a fixed reed, a loose-fitting plastic reed is exposed in the mouthpiece. The reed is inserted into the mouth and, depending upon where pressure is applied along the length of the reed, the pitch can easily be changed. Open-reed calls are extremely versatile. They can produce sounds that mimic mice and other small rodents all the way up to fawn bleats simply by changing the position of the reed and the volume of air. Also, they don't freeze up. I've used them in below-zero conditions and have not had any difficulty with them. When the reed is placed inside your mouth it instantly separates, allowing air to pass through.

The one disadvantage of the open-reed call is that it's harder to learn to use. For a new predator caller, it's not as simple to pick up and blow as a closed-reed call. However, once mastered, it's hard to beat a quality open-reed call for sound variety and versatility.

Howlers

The howler is another type of mouth call that's useful at times. Generally of open-reed construction (I've seen some closed-reed types), they take a bit of practice to get used to.

I use a howler at three specific times. The first is when I'm trying to locate a coyote. If I'm hunting unknown country and a coyote could be in one of many draws or valleys, I howl before entering the area. Depending upon the response, I can set up accordingly, move closer or, in the case of no response, sometimes go to another area entirely.

The locating howl consists of two barks followed by a long, drawn-out howl. Don't worry if you don't get a response immediately; many times, the response doesn't come for several minutes. If you believe you're in a good area but there's no response, set up and call anyway, as coyotes don't always respond to a howl.

The second time I howl is during mating/denning time, which takes place in the early spring throughout the U.S. During this time, coyotes pair up and become very territorial. A challenge howl or bark will often elicit a response from any coyote in the area, which will then come to investigate who is in his territory.

The other time I howl – and it's more of a bark than a howl – is when I want a coyote to stop. If a coyote is coming fast to a distress call and there is a good chance he will overrun the caller or get in a bad position for a shot, I issue one or two short choppy barks. This will generally bring the animal to an abrupt stop, looking right at you, so it's a good idea to shoulder your gun before making this call. If multiples come to a call, and a shot is fired, more than likely any unwounded coyote will instantly be off for parts unknown. A wounded bark will

Howlers can make a big difference when blind-calling an area or hunting aggressive coyotes in the spring.

sometimes cause a runner to stop to see what happened. It doesn't always work, but it has worked often enough that I carry a small open-reed howler and use it if the opportunity presents itself.

Custom Calls

Custom calls are more of a style than a distinct type of call. I have custom closed-reed calls, open-reed calls and howlers. A custom call is simply one precisely manufactured, one at a time and often to the buyer's specific requirements. Currently my favorite custom predator-call manufacturer is Ryan Wieser of R.A.W. calls. His woodworking ability is awesome and all of his calls are handtuned before they leave his shop. While they cost substantially more than an off-the-shelf production call, they often sound much better and are works of art.

Bulb Calls

Bulb calls, (often called squeakers) are handy in any successful predator caller's arsenal. Designed much like a pet's squeaky toy, it's a small closed-reed call inserted into a flexible plastic or rubber bulb, much like a turkey baster. When compressed, the bulb forces air through the reed, emitting a small sound. While I don't use one as a primary call, they do have several advantages. First, they don't freeze up since no moist air is passing between the reed and body. Second, they're simple and easy to use. Third, they require minimal move-

RAW Custom Calls are the some of the nicest examples of fine custom calls.

A selection of custom calls.

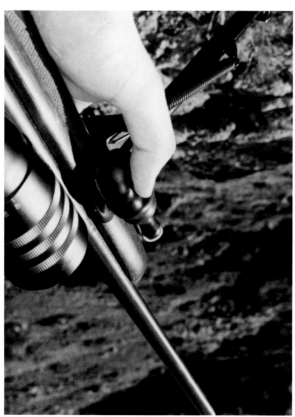

Attaching a bulb call to the forearm of your rifle with Velcro, double-sided tape or even a rubber band makes for convenient calling when a predator is looking your way.

ment to operate. This is extremely important when a predator has already zeroed in on your position and any movement will spook him. I generally keep a squeaker close at hand when calling, either attached to my weapon or inserted inside the pocket portion of my glove/mitts, where it's easy to grasp. In this fashion, I can have my rifle shouldered and still coax a predator into final range without moving.

Electronic Callers

Electronic callers are nothing new. In fact the first versions, produced by Johnny Stewart, have been around since 1961. In the last 10 years they have exploded onto the scene with many new technological advancements. Electronic callers come in many shapes and sizes, but share similar advantages. They allow a caller to reproduce perfect-sounding calls regardless of skill level. They can often be louder than standard mouth calls, depending upon the unit. They also provide a caller with a large number of different sounds, some of which are extremely hard to make with mouth calls. Finally, electronic calls can be remotely used, which removes the sounds from the vicinity of the hunter and provides more freedom of movement with less chance of being spotted. To those who have considered purchasing one, a disadvantage is obvious: They're much more costly than traditional mouth calls. They're also much heavier to tote afield.

Electronic callers work great and produce many sounds that are difficult to make with a mouth call.

CD or Tape?

Several manufacturers offer tape or CD electronic callers, and the main two are Johnny Stewart and Lohman. Both companies produce high-quality units, and a prospective buyer can rest assured with either one. In my opinion, CDs sound better than tapes, especially at higher volumes. They're more sensitive to field conditions, however. Dirt and dust are not too compatible with delicate instruments. That being said, I've used a Lohman CD predator caller for the better part of two seasons, and with normal care have not experienced any problems with it.

Digital

This last season I used the Fox Pro Digital caller with great results. Styled after a conventional 6-volt flashlight, this unit is ideal for a variety of applications. It's small and lightweight, and the batteries have more than enough juice for a day's worth of calling. With a choice of several different prerecorded wildlife sounds, changing from a cottontail squeal to a coyote howl is as simple as turning a knob. While this unit has about everything I've been looking for in an electronic caller, it does have one drawback – price. It costs a bit more than a standard electronic tape player. But if convenience and quality is a concern, it's hard to beat this product.

The battery-operated Fox Pro Digital caller resembles a flashlight

The Phantom call is another digital option, and it's about a simple as a caller can get. It has a touch pad and a remote speaker – that's it. The entire unit operates off a 9-volt battery. One feature I really like about this caller is that it will play different sounds simultaneously. For example, a hunter can have a cottontail in distress with an occasional coyote howling over the wailing rabbit. The Phantom also produces sounds that are extremely difficult to make with a mouth call, such as a lamb bleat.

Out West, jackrabbits are one of a coyote's prime food sources. Mimic their cry of distress and watch what unfolds.

Sounds for Different Predators

Coyotes – Whether they're from birds, rabbits, mice or fawns, the sounds of animals in distress all have a similar, plaintive quality. The pitch, tone and frequency varies, but the meaning is still there: "I am hurting and not long for this world." Being first and foremost opportunistic hunters, coyotes can't resist responding to these calls. While 90 percent of the time I use either a jackrabbit or cottontail-in-distress call, I've called coyotes in using bird sounds, rodent squeaks, fawn bleats and, around suburban areas, one of the most disturbing sounds I've ever heard – the "kitten-in-distress" tape.

Foxes – While all of the standard distress calls work well for coyotes, I find myself calling softer with a higher pitch for foxes. Calls like the rodent squeak and bird in distress have produced the best results for me when fox hunting. During certain times of the year, fox-pup distress calls also work extremely well.

Bobcats – With bobcats, softer is often better. They will respond to the loud wailing of a rabbit call, but I've found that less is more in most cases. Try using a short- to medium-range rabbit squall in a soft tone. I also like to use short rodent squeaks. The key to calling bobcats is patience. If you are accustomed to coyotes bounding onto the scene a few minutes after the notes leave the call, you will be disappointed by bobcats. On the other hand, if you have patience and believe a cat is stalking your position, the thrill of seeing a feline face poking from a clump of grass 20 yards away after 45 minutes of calling is hard to beat.

Bears and Cougars – There is no doubt that the large predators are attracted to mammal-in-distress calls. Even though bears and cougars are on the top of the food chain, at the right time of the year (late fall), a rabbit-in-distress call may bring them running. However, there are better calls for the task. Cougars and bears like big meals, and nothing is quite as irresistible as a fawn or calf elk bleat. Both of these sounds mean a large meal that is relatively easy to catch. In the case of a hungry bear, expect a fast run into the call – much like a 300-pound coyote! A cougar is stealthy like a bobcat and will slink in to size up the situation before fully committing. In either case, the thrill will be second to none.

Calling When Conditions Get Tough

When I awoke in the icy winter darkness to the sound of my alarm, I could hear the wind rustling the dead leaves outside my window. When I got dressed and fired up the truck, the wind was gusting regularly. By

For a serious predator hunter, rough weather is all in a day's work.

the time my partner and I finally got to our first stand of the morning, the wind was no longer gusting but blowing at a steady clip. I wish I could say it died down with the sunrise, but later that day I caught myself reminiscing about the "relative calm" of the predawn light.

Wind can be a predator caller's worst enemy. It can eddy and swirl, spreading scent and making setups unpredictable. It can gust so hard, calls cannot be heard, and animals refuse to move, choosing to spend the day holed up in a sheltered place. A predator hunter has two choices during these times: either spend the day at home by the fire, or hunt despite the wind. It's always been my opinion that as long as I'm afield, I've got a chance of success; if I'm at home, there's no chance at all.

Because of this philosophy, and because I live in Nebraska where the wind is almost a constant presence, I've learned to cope with it. Here are a few tricks I've picked up along the way:

When the wind is blowing, look for spots tucked out of the wind, such as draws and gullies with plenty of small trees and brush.

Photo by David Draper

Go Loud or Go Home

During one windy hunting day, my partner and I approached a small rise overlooking a large valley floor. He proceeded to crest the ridge, while I stayed on the backside slope to cover the back door. We were no more than 50 yards apart, and it was his turn to call on this stand. I sat down, lowered my bipod and waited . . .

. . . and waited and waited. No sound came from his position. After five minutes, I figured something was wrong. He was either pinned down by a coyote or something had happened, but I decided to give it another few minutes before going to investigate. Suddenly, a muffled "crack" of a rifle interrupted the sound of the wind. After a few minutes of silence, I went to investigate. My partner was halfway down the slope dragging a dead coyote behind him.

"Shortly after the second calling sequence, this dog appeared out of nowhere and came right in," he explained. " I shot him around 75 yards away."

"The second calling sequence? I never heard you call at all." I said incredulously.

It was then I realized how much effect the wind has on sound. Luckily, the coyote must have been bedded really close or he would have never heard the call.

Most callers have been told that coyotes and foxes can hear sounds up to a mile away. I'm sure that on a calm, cold day, this is probably true. In fact, I think they can hear even farther. However, when the wind is howling, I believe the average call can be heard between 100-300 yards, depending upon the intensity and direction of the wind, the volume of the call and the amount of background noise such as rustling leaves and branches.

Calling with the Wind

The golden rule of picking a calling spot is to make sure you're calling with the wind in your face or slightly diagonal to your position. This is a good rule to follow, but on really windy days, sometimes you have no other option than to call with the wind. If it's steady and constantly coming from one direction, positioning yourself on the downside of a small rise or at the head of a draw and calling with the wind will ensure the sound carries a long way.

Sound isn't the only thing the wind carries, however; your scent is carried, too. But if certain precautions are taken, successfully tagging a coyote or fox can be a real possibility even when you're calling with the wind.

When I head out to call predators on windy days, I look more like a serious whitetail hunter than I do a dedicated predator caller. I shower and wash my hair with Robinson Labs' scent-eliminating soap, then I wear a full suit of their Scent Blocker clothing (including gloves and face mask). This obviously won't eliminate all human scent, but reduces it to levels undetectable to a predator's sharp nose until the animal is in range and it's too late.

During these situations, I use a two-call approach. I begin with a close-range squeaker to see if there are any predators laid up with 100 yards or so. If nothing shows after two or three calling sessions of a minute each, I use the loudest call I have — in most cases, a large-diameter, open-reed call.

Electronic calls often work well in the wind. Many are extremely loud, and when combined with the right tape, can cover a lot more range than many mouth calls. While I am lazy and don't really care to lug the extra weight of an electric call around all day, during windy days, I often find myself with an electric call.

Hunting Protected Areas

Predators, for the most part, don't like being out in gale-force winds any more than you do. They can't hear well, they expend significant amounts of energy through heat loss, and there are not many prey species available as they, too, are hunkered down. Predators seek shelter and protection from the storm and often spend the entire day holed up. This protection will always be as far out of the wind as possible. It might be a rocky outcropping, a brush-choked ravine or even the lee side of a hill or a rise.

This is often close-range calling, and if a predator is going to respond, it will appear sooner than later. The key to this type of hunting is to sneak into their "home" undetected, and then call softly. Keep your calling sessions short – only three or four quick bursts – and then get ready. If nothing responds in a minute or two, repeat the sequence four to five times. If nothing shows up in 10 minutes, move to a new location.

This type of hunting does not require that you move very far. For example, on calm days when I know my calls are really reaching out, I usually move at least a mile between calling sites. But for "micro" hunting on windy days, I may just walk over the rise into the next brush-choked basin. The next stand can be as close as 300 yards from the previous one, depending upon terrain and intensity of the wind.

While I feel naked afield without a rifle, depending upon the terrain, these protected areas are perfect spots for scatterguns. Often the shots are at close range at moving targets. Countless times I've had a coyote see me at the same time I saw him and had to take a running shot. Out to 40 yards, a 12 gauge with a heavy load of BBs is ideal.

Multiple 'Yotes Are Possible

On a calm day after I pull the trigger on one dog, I generally only make a half-hearted attempt to keep calling for a second coyote. In an area with a high coyote population density, I've had successive coyotes come in after the shot, but it's rare. However, on windy days the report from a rifle, like the noise from a call, does not carry very far. For this reason, I believe I've had much better success calling in multiple dogs on windy days. So after the shot, keep calling and scanning the area for at least another 10 minutes; you never know what may appear.

Choosing the Right Rifle

After calling a predator into range, the next part of the equation is making the shot. Windy days present their own set of difficulties for rifles as well as calls. I do a lot of my hunting with a .17 Remington. Loaded with the right bullets, and by keeping the shots under 250 yards, it completely pole axes predators up to and including coyotes with minimal pelt damage. However, when the wind is howling around the eaves, I dig into the back of the gun safe for my windy-day coyote rifle. My pet coyote rifle for windy conditions is a Weatherby SPM chambered in .243 Winchester, loaded with wind-bucking VLD (Very Low Drag) bullets. This rifle will take coyotes out to 250 yards in the midst of a storm.

All bullets are deflected by wind, the degree of which is dictated by total bullet weight, profile and velocity. Obviously, some bullets/calibers are better than others. In the wind, my pet .17 is about worthless for anything over 100 yards away. All .22 centerfires, from .222s to .22-250s also suffer greatly from wind drift at longer ranges. While they will work, when the wind really starts to howl, larger calibers with specially designed low-drag bullets are the best solution. I personally like the .243 caliber, as it's accurate, performs well and has low enough recoil to maintain target acquisition after the shot. However, I've also used .270s and .300 Win Mags, and they worked well despite the added recoil and additional pelt damage.

When Not to Hunt

As much as I hate to admit it, there are times when I don't hunt when the wind is blowing. If the wind is constantly switching and swirling, many of these techniques become useless. In addition, sometimes more damage than good is done by going out. If you only have a few good areas and you hunt them in the wind, you're probably going to educate some coyotes. In my opinion, these spots should be saved for a perfect day. Hunt your least-productive spots on windy days. However, if you hunt in an area that has more prime spots than could be covered in a lifetime of hunting, the damage probably won't be significant.

9

Decoys for Success

When a coyote is uncommitted, sometimes all it takes to seal the deal is the enticing movement of a decoy.

W e'd been on stand for less than five minutes when the coyote appeared like a glistening white orb on the distant rise some 400 yards away. It's a sight I never tire of seeing. One moment there was nothing as I turned my head back and forth surveying the country, when suddenly there he was. Full-furred and splendid, he stood there mirroring my gaze, looking for danger while at the same time searching for what was making all the racket. This was going to be a dead dog if he decided to come any closer.

He just stood there looking, however – even a few quiet squeaks went unacknowledged. My partner and I sat motionless, not wanting to give him any reason for alarm, confident in our camo, our setup, the wind direction and calling. But still he stayed there, looking the area over.

I called softly again, and once more he stared in our direction. Not seeing anything after a few minutes, he went back to surveying the countryside. After about 10 minutes, he laid down. No amount of calling would allay his suspicion as he lay basking in the morning sun. Looking at my partner, I gave a small shrug, which

This stubborn coyote changed his mind and came on a dead run once he saw the Predator Supreme Decoy.

implied, "What now?" He shrugged back and made an imaginary pistol with his right hand. I shrugged again and gave him a thumbs up.

It was an extremely low-percentage shot, even though there was no wind. I don't like needlessly educating coyotes to calling, but unless we wanted to sit there all day and wait for him to leave, we were going to have to try a shot. Attempting to sneak away would likely educate him.

I looked over at my partner. He was peering through the scope on his Remington 700 .22-250 as it rested on the Harris bipod. Holding up one finger as a sign to wait a minute, I barked loudly through my howler. The coyote stood up from his prone position, walked around in a full circle and sat down facing us. For a long-range, low-percentage shot, a coyote sitting and facing the shooter is the best possibility as it offers the most room for vertical error. I now gave him the thumbs up and watched through my scope to call the shot. I don't know how high he aimed, but it wasn't enough. At the shot, the dirt erupted between the coyote's two front feet. He flipped a reverse somersault in midair that would have made an Olympic gymnast proud, then crested the ridge with his tail between his

legs. My partner had performed well under the circumstances, but the end result was the same: No coyote in the bag, but another extremely well educated one.

We talked it over as we headed back to the truck. It was evident that the coyote had been shot at before; he was just too wary. He never saw or smelled us – that I'm confident of. He just didn't see anything to confirm what his ears were telling him. In most cases, coyotes rely on their hearing and consequently are fooled into gun range. It was my guess that he'd trusted his ears once too often in the past. "Oh well," I said. "You win some and you lose some" and headed to the next stand.

This stand also started off well. We had a coyote trotting toward us within the first five minutes. When as he closed to within 300 yards, though, his intentions became obvious: He began making a sweeping turn that would place him directly downwind, about 200 yards away. Before he could get there, my partner issued a short, quick, challenge bark with his howler. The coyote put the brakes on at around 250 yards and stared in our direction.

I already had my rifle shouldered and I squeezed off a shot, hitting him a bit far back but close enough

Call-shy coyotes often hold up just out of range and stare at the caller's position until they see something that confirms what their ears are telling them.

to count. As we walked out to collect the prize, my partner commented on how spooky these coyotes were. I had to agree. While this was a good spot, I knew it offered easy access and was heavily hunted. It also was open desert where a struggling prey animal could easily be seen. We figured we needed something to draw the coyote's attention and hopefully convince it to close the deal. At that time, there were no commercial decoys readily available, so we decided to try to make our own.

Our first attempt consisted of a wadded-up ball of newspaper with a rabbit skin wrapped over it and stapled in place. From it, we tied a 20-yard length of monofilament that we could tug on to make it move. Our plan was to hang this decoy over fence lines, branches and sagebrush and tug on the line when a coyote came into sight. To our surprise, it worked. Sometimes coyotes never noticed it, but for others that needed convincing, it seemed to satisfy their curiosity and made them believe the setup was real.

Today, there are several commercially made predator decoys that work in most situations, and I choose to leave the ball of newspaper and line behind. The new models perform so well and are so easy to use, they're hard for predators to resist. Although I don't use them every time, I do use them when the country is extremely open or hard-hunted. I also find decoys indispensable for solo hunting and bowhunting.

When Alone, Bring a Decoy

When you're by yourself, it's difficult to cover every avenue of approach. A coyote can slip in the back door and check out the area, often spotting your movements in the process. Recently I went out to one of my honey holes for a quick calling session before work. Essentially a large horseshoe of badlands and eroded rock complete with crevasses and holes, this large canyon has little in the way of brushy cover, but is perfect coyote and bobcat habitat.

Because I could not cover all of the approach areas, I placed my Predator Supreme decoy 20 yards in front of me in a patch of short cheatgrass, and nestled down among the rocks. After 10 minutes of calling, I figured nothing was in the canyon, but decided to stick it out for another 10 minutes. Just then, I heard a few pebbles slide down the rock face behind me. I slowly turned my head and saw two coyotes poised on the brink of a rock ledge, peering at the struggling decoy. They were both less then 10 yards away and had approached from an angle that left me completely exposed. If their attention had not been fixed on the decoy, they would have surely caught my head movements. They came down the rock face, eyes locked onto the decoy. I managed to swivel 180 degrees around and shoot the second coyote as he came past. The first escaped through the boulder field. If I'd been using a shotgun, I could have dragged two coyotes home that morning, but a single coyote is better than none at all.

Place your decoy in a position where it will be seen. Open, relatively high spots are ideal.

Decoys for Primitive-Weapons Hunting

When hunting coyotes with short-range weapons (a shotgun, pistol, muzzleloader or bow), a decoy is almost a necessity. When a coyote is within 50 yards and hears your call, he can pinpoint your location to the inch. But if you can get his attention with the decoy when he's still 100 yards or so out, you can pretty much quit calling and allow him to come in on sight alone.

A decoy also allows you to get away with a lot of movement. This is especially important when drawing a bow. Ideally, you want to draw when the coyote is out of sight in a low spot or obstructed by cover. I've drawn on coyotes while they were in plain view and can tell you it's a lot easier to do when their attention is fixed on what they think is a struggling bunny.

Decoys can be as simple as a feather flapping in the breeze.

George Brint, inventor of the Predator Supreme decoy, with another fooled coyote.

In heavy cover, I like to elevate my decoys to a place where approaching coyotes will have a better chance of seeing them. In the West, barbed-wire fencelines work great for this purpose.

Decoying Cats

While a decoy works well for certain coyote hunting situations, it works great for calling cats. Cats, both bobcats and cougars, don't respond to calling like coyotes do. Cats are cautious and quietly sneak into a setup, fully surveying the surrounding areas before making a pounce. They often slink into shooting range without the hunter knowing it. They remain crouched, looking the situation over until they either see the hunter and quietly sneak away, or the hunter figures nothing is coming and stands up, blowing the whole situation. However, if a cat sees the object that's making all the commotion, he will focus his attention on it and make a final stalk, often providing a shot.

Since deer are a cougar's main dinner item, fawn decoys are ideal for hunting the large North American cat. Setting up on cougars can be like decoying any other predator. Work with whatever terrain is available. I've called cougars in the dense undergrowth of western Washington rain forests and have found that hunting from a climbing stand is the best method. You can overlook your decoy and see through the surrounding growth much better than when sitting on the ground.

Types of Decoys

Decoy Heart Predator Supreme

This is a relatively new decoy, and to my way of think-ing is one of the best. It's simple to use, easy to carry afield and is versatile. Sure, it looks like nothing real, but when you get back 100 yards, it looks a lot like everything. It has rabbit-colored hair and moves realistically. I believe that's all a coyote needs to be convinced. It's easily carried in a day-pack and can be deployed for instant use. The key to its movement is a "decoy heart" motion ball under the faux-fur covering. A twist of the switch and the unit bounces erratically on a spring secured to a ground stake. It runs off one AA battery that lasts for several hours of continuous use.

I like this decoy, not only for its good looks, but also because of its versatility. In open country, it can be stuck into a clearing, but in the waist-high sagebrush where I often find myself hunting, it's simple to hang the unit by its long tail from a tall bush or the top strand of a barbed-wire fence. The decoy then bounces and vibrates several feet from the ground and is easy to see by any approaching coyote.

Recently I talked with George Brint, inventor of the Predator Supreme Decoy, to get some of his thoughts on using a decoy.

"I first started using a decoy in 1992," Brint recalls. "Then it was just a makeshift one – actually a stuffed dog toy. It worked great, but only when a coyote saw it. I realized that without movement, it was severely lacking. That's when I decided to incorporate movement, and it made all the difference in the world. The Predator Supreme is mounted on a stake with a spring, has a Decoy

Some decoys are so lifelike, they appear real — but is all the realism necessary?

Heart and has a long, limber tail. Movement is the key. When I used to call without a decoy, my average success rate was around 45 percent. Now it's above 80 percent. A decoy can make this much of a difference."

Brint explains how he uses his decoy. "I try to sit in front of a honeysuckle, cedar or brushline to break up my outline. I don't try to hide, but sit in shade and try to blend and be as still as possible. I put the decoy about 50 to 60 yards out with a couple of squirts of fox or coon urine around it. After turning it on and getting settled in my position, I start calling as normal, with one exception: Once I see a coyote, I quit calling and let him lock on to the decoy. At this point, the call has done its job and the decoy takes over. Typically, a coyote will approach within 20 to 50 yards of the decoy and then stop, as if to say 'What's this?' That's when I take the shot."

Rigor Rabbit

This foam rabbit/prairie dog decoy works well in open areas. Although it doesn't have the versatility of the Predator Supreme decoy, it does create a good illusion and a lot of lifelike movement. The enticing motion of the decoy will work equally well on cats and coyotes. What I didn't like about this decoy was the cumbersome base and somewhat delicate foam "rabbit."

Feather Flex Fawn

This decoy is the ultimate for cougar and even bobcat hunting. It's made from collapsible foam, so it can easily be tucked into a daypack. It has the correct size and stance to entice wary predators into committing to a stand. This decoy, combined with a fawn-in-distress call, could create some exciting action from bears as well. The foam construction is similar to the Rigor Rabbit, but since this decoy needs to be carried in a separate pack or turkey vest, tearing the material is not a problem.

Custom-Manufactured and Homemade Decoys

There are several manufacturers that make custom decoys out of fully taxidermied rabbit mounts. These mounts vary in quality, and some of the better ones even sit on a fake rock and are capable of some vertical movement. (I've used two kinds. One was operated by a pull string; the other ran off batteries.) They do work, and I've tried them on several outings. The biggest complaint I had with them was that they're fragile and hard to carry afield. Yes, they look extremely lifelike, but does that make them a better attractor than an imitation like a Rigor Rabbit or Predator Supreme? I personally don't think so, at least not enough to justify the extra effort.

Think about it. How closely does a Light Cahill dry fly resemble an actual mayfly, or the average duck caller sound like a real duck? Impression is what we're trying to sell. A decoy does not have to be so detailed that it can stand close scrutiny. If it's small, brown, acts wounded and a coyote could get it into his mouth, odds are it will work.

And what about the newspaper and old rabbit skin trick? Will it still fool a predator? I'll bet dollars to doughnuts it will. I haven't tried it in a few years, but there's no reason it won't work as well now as it did then. But with so many great and inexpensive options on the market today, it seems silly to be tugging the end of a string tied to a newspaper in hope that a coyote will notice.

10

Predator Guns & Accessories

I've often been asked, "How do you select the right gun for predator hunting?" The answer is simple: You choose one like you would for any other type of hunting. You pick the one that best meets the requirements of the job. In fact, you may already have a gun for other uses that will work just fine. Certainly over the years, more small- and medium-size predators have been killed with the lowly .22 caliber rimfire than any other cartridge. And more bears and cougars have been shot by someone's deer rifle than a gun chosen especially for the task.

The requirements of a predator rifle can be easily summarized:
- It must be powerful enough to make positive, humane kills.
- It must be accurate enough to consistently hit the target at the ranges expected.
- It must be portable enough to be easily carried and handled in a hunting situation.
- It must be rugged enough to withstand the conditions in which it will be exposed.
- It should be comfortable and familiar to the shooter so he can handle it well in the field.
- It satisfies the personal preferences of the shooter.

Actions

The heart of any rifle is the action. Between my own experience and that of my hunting partners, I've seen about every type of action employed for predators. Levers, pumps, semiautos, rolling blocks, falling blocks, break-opens, bolts – all have been used with success. So, type of action pretty much becomes a matter of personal opinion and preference. However, some do serve the purpose bet-

Predator rifles come in all shapes and sizes. Pick the one that best suits your needs and requirements, and you'll be happy.

Many different types of actions will work, but bolt-action rifles are by far the most commonly used for predator hunting.

ter than others, and seeing all these different rifles in use over the years has molded my opinion on what makes a good predator rifle.

For hunting smaller predators (coyotes, foxes and bobcats), accuracy is an important consideration. The targets are diminutive and the ranges can be long. Many different action types can produce good accuracy, but few do it as well or consistently as a good bolt action. In addition to being accurate, bolt actions are simple, trouble-free, easy to use, provide simple mounting for telescopic sights, and most hold several shells. There are numerous makes and models to choose from. Almost every manufacturer has at least one bolt action in their line. For all of these reasons, I find myself carrying a bolt-action rifle more often than not.

However, there are exceptions. For bear and mountain lion hunting, especially when dogs are used, a fast-handling lever action or carbine semiauto is easy to carry all day and slips nicely into a saddle scabbard when hunting from horseback. Accuracy is less important than portability and fast handling. Shots are often closer than 50 yards at a target much larger than a coyote.

Special Conditions

Always consider any special conditions you may encounter. For example, I learned a valuable and costly lesson on a recent spring bear hunt in coastal Alaska. Constant rain, salt spray and bouncing around in a metal boat will quickly wreak havoc on beautiful wood and blued steel. Whether you consider them aesthetically ugly

or not, synthetic stocks and stainless steel are valuable for this type of hunting.

Other things to take into account may include the rigors of off-road travel, availability of non-standard ammunition, extreme fluctuations in temperature and humidity, and access to parts or repair for uncommon firearms.

Accuracy

Rifle accuracy is ever evolving. Twenty-five years ago, it took a serious custom rifle with lots of judicious hand-loading to get minute-of-angle groups. MOA roughly equals 1 inch at 100 yards, 2 inches at 200, and so on. Today, many shooters are not satisfied with rifles that won't do MOA "out of the box" with factory ammo. Fortunately, most of them will! Due to better barrel machining, tighter action tolerances, more stable synthetic stocks and other advancements, manufacturers today are consistently turning out rifles that will place five shots under a quarter at 100 yards – impressive indeed!

If the truth be known, almost any well-made rifle in good condition using high-quality factory ammunition will shoot straighter than the gunner is able to achieve under field hunting conditions.

How accurate does a predator rifle need to be? Regardless of where I hunt or the species pursued, from prairie dogs to elk, I feel comfortable with a minute-of-angle rifle. One inch at 100 yards is really all that's needed to cleanly take any animal. Beyond that, tweaking for accuracy becomes an obsession and an end in itself rather

In areas that get a lot of rain, stainless rifles may be the best choice.

than a hunting requirement. But aren't tighter groups better? I would say no, but allow me to explain.

It's been my experience as a three-position rifle competitor, coach and rangemaster that an average hunter at 100 yards can shoot 2-inch groups prone, 4-inch groups sitting, 6-inch groups kneeling and is lucky to keep all his shots on target while shooting offhand! Combine this with wind and a moving target, and it's easy to see that an additional half-inch in rifle accuracy plays a very insignificant role in the life and death of a coyote.

If killing more predators is your goal, sight your rifle 1.5 inches high at 100 yards, make sure it is consistently shooting MOA, and then spend the rest of your time at the range shooting from unsupported positions. Few people today practice actual riflemanship; instead they rely on mechanical rifle accuracy, superior optics and shooting supports. When afield, I always try to shoot from some type of rest, whether it's a commercial bipod or a rolled-up jacket over my pack. There are times when a predator catches you off guard and you have to shoot from either a standing or kneeling position. Only practice will help you make the shot.

Predator Rifles vs. Varmint Rifles

There's a major difference between hunting varmints (prairie dogs, groundhogs, crows, etc.) and hunting predators. Taking predators is a hunting game in all aspects. Taking varmints is basically a shooting game, usually at long ranges and at relatively stationary targets.

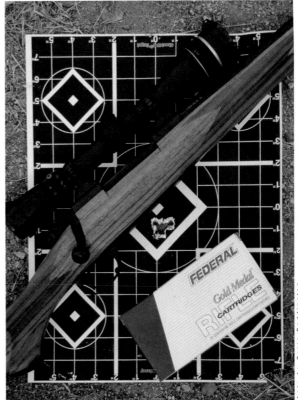

Predator rifles need to be accurate, but how much accuracy is enough? Most serious predator hunters agree that Minute of Angle is all that's really required for most situations.

Varmint and predator are not interchangeable terms when it comes to choosing a rifle. A predator hunter wants a rifle that is fast-handling and easy to carry, but still accurate.

One of my first varmint rifles was a bull-barreled Remington 700 in .22-250. It was a fine rifle that shot half-inch groups with a variety of ammo. I saved my pennies for a summer and topped it off with enough glass to choke a horse — a Nightforce 8x-32x. I felt I had the ultimate predator-shooting machine. The rifle was accurate and consistent, and the Hubbell-like scope had good light-gathering ability and enough magnification to to see to the end of the county. It would have been a perfect prairie dog/varmint rifle, but it turned out to be a lousy predator rifle. My first trip to the eastern Washington desert left me sweating and my shoulder aching – this overweight monstrosity was not a stalking rifle. It really needed a set of wheels.

On the first day of the hunt, after touting all the qualities of the rifle to my hunting partner, we had our first coyote come in. In typical desert fashion, he was nearly in our lap before the first notes were done echoing from the call. I shouldered the rifle for an absurdly easy 50-yard chip shot, only to realize that the scope had been left on 32x from the last stand, and the parallax adjustment was set at 150 yards. The scope was entirely out of focus. It was like looking through a lens coated with Vaseline. I slowly reached forward and cranked the scope down to 8x. By the time I looked up, the coyote had seen the movements and was trotting off at a quick clip through the dense sagebrush. Throwing the rifle to my shoulder, all I could see was pieces of fur as he sped away. I squeezed off a shot at a section of fur that I hoped might cover some vitals, but the bullet failed to connect, and he kicked it into high gear and was gone. The rifle and scope was up for sale the following week. I learned the hard way that a predator rifle and a varmint rifle are two distinctly different things.

What are the differences between a predator rifle and a varmint rifle? For hunting varmints, you need a rifle that's flat-shooting, features a bull barrel (to enhance accuracy and be more consistent during extended shooting sessions), and have optics of around 20x or more. A typical varmint rifle may be shot several hundred times in a day on a good prairie-dog field. The small targets will be relatively stationary, but at long range.

A typical predator rifle is shot a few times a day, but must be carried great distances. Shots may be at moving targets. Often, the shots are less than 100 yards at a relatively large target. A standard sporter-weight production rifle should provide all the accuracy that's required. I don't like carrying the extra weight of a heavy barrel when I don't need the additional accuracy. There's little need for high-power optics (over 20x). Most predators coming to a call present a shot under 100 yards. For most predator rifles, a 4x-14x scope with good light-gathering capabilities is ideal.

The terms get used synonymously, but the differences between a varmint rifle and predator rifle are considerable.

Today's modern "turkey" shotguns work well for predators. They're light, easy to swing and come in matte or camo finishes.

Craig Boddington on Predator Rifles and Calibers

I asked noted hunting author and rifleman Craig Boddington what makes a good predator rifle as well as his favorite caliber. For such a complex question, I got a pretty straightforward answer.

"A good predator rifle needs to be reasonably accurate, but above all it needs to be fast-handling, because when calling, you never know what kind of shot you might get.

"In open country, there is a strong argument that an accurate .22-250 is probably the best choice, but a .22-250 has some disadvantages as well. If a lot of shooting is to be encountered, a sporter-weight .22-250 heats up too fast and the bullets are overly destructive on bobcats and foxes. So my personal favorite all-around predator rifle is a sporter-weight .223 loaded with 50-grain bullets, which cause less pelt damage than the lighter, faster slugs.

"Concerning bears, I have a tremendous respect for black bears, so I like to use reasonably heavy calibers with big bullets that hit hard and provide absolute penetration. My favorites are the medium-velocity .35s, from the .348, .356 and .358 Winchester up to the .350 Remington and .35 Whelen."

In heavy cover, multiple projectiles are often better than one.

Shotguns for Predators

I grew up in the rain forest of western Washington, where long-range shooting and great visibility did not exist. The average shot on anything from grouse to bears was almost always under 20 yards. Calling coyotes and bobcats in this green, rain-soaked jungle often brought shots that were much closer and came very fast. Using a fast-handling shotgun for this type of hunting was an obvious choice. I rarely called coyotes while carrying a rifle – there were simply too few advantages and many disadvantages. It was not until I moved away to college in the eastern part of the state, where sagebrush and rolling wheat fields replaced stands of cedar trees, that I started regularly hunting coyotes with a rifle. Even then, I probably would have done better with a shotgun in certain situations.

This country was open to the extreme. It was quite easy to see the curvature of the horizon. I always carried a flat-shooting rifle topped with large optics. On most open-country stands, it worked fine, but often I found myself calling in little brush-choked gullies and rocky draws. There were so many coyotes in this region that often two or three would come in together. I honestly don't believe they'd ever been called (at least not very much). Farm hands would stop their pickups and shoot at any coyote in sight, but few went out hunting them.

There was little hesitation with these animals, and multiples responding to a call were common. Many times I'd make one call, stop short, drop my call in my lap and snap-shoot at a coyote as he burned up a draw less than 25 yards away. At that distance, all I could see was fur in the scope. Then it dawned on me – even though the country was open and it looked like I should be carrying a rifle, most of my shots were at the same distance as back home. Why not carry a shotgun? After giving the matter some thought, I did eventually carry a shotgun, along with a rifle. I kept the shotgun in my lap for those close-range, fast-approaching dogs and a rifle on a bipod next to me for times when they hung up out of shotgun range.

If you're hunting with a partner, one can use a rifle while the other carries a shotgun. Set up to give the rifle shooter the best lanes of fire for distance shots, while the hunter with the shotgun covers the "back door" or the bottom of a small ravine or other likely looking depressions.

What Makes a Good Predator Shotgun?

Any 12-gauge waterfowling or upland bird hunting piece will work adequately for predator hunting. But the new generation of "turkey" shotguns is ideal. They're short-barreled, which makes them fast and easy to handle in the woods as well as for snap-shooting running coyotes and foxes. They're camouflaged or matte-finished to elim-

In mixed terrain, a combination rifle/shotgun sometimes makes for a perfect predator gun.

inate shine. Most come with a sling for ease of transport afield. In addition to the three-dot fiber optic sights, which make target acquisition (even in low light) a breeze, they have an extended extra-full choke that will throw dense enough patterns with the right lead load to reliably kill coyotes, foxes and bobcats to 50 yards. They're available in pump, single-shot and autoloading actions, but I would stick to either a pump or autoloader, as the multiple shots will be appreciated when a pair of coyotes respond to a call. Kept clean and properly lubricated, either will function in the worst of conditions, with a slight mechanical edge going to the pump action.

Alternative Weaponry

When I was in college, I spent most of the fall hunting pheasants. In addition to the great upland gunning, it would be a rare day when we would not kick a coyote out of a brush patch. The coyotes seemed to always know we were after birds, and not them. They would usually stop about 100 yards away and just stare, like they knew that a load of lead 5s at 100 yards is pretty poor and ineffective coyote medicine.

One day, a partner and I headed afield for a day of bird shooting. When we reached our spot, I noticed he had a different gun case in the back of the pickup. To my surprise, not only was it a different case, but a different gun entirely. It was a Savage over-and-under combo rifle/shotgun, chambered in .223/12 gauge. The ideal upland bird/coyote gun was born. Actually, I learned later in life that we were not the first to discover the superb functionality of a rifle and a shotgun combined into one shooting piece. Referred to as drillings, combos or cape guns, these firearms have been around pretty much since gun makers figured out that multiple barrels could be soldered together.

The model my hunting partner carried was a very utilitarian piece designed for functionality over grace and looks. But it did work, and not only did he bag many birds, he also surprised a few coyotes as well.

Shooting Supports

Shooting supports will greatly improve a hunter's capability in the field. These fall into many categories, from commercial bipods to something as simple as a rolled-up jacket over a rocky outcropping. There are several good portable shooting supports available that are ideal for predator hunters.

Bipods

Bipods are made by several manufacturers, and all are slightly different. Here are some things I prefer in a bipod. First is convenience. A bipod needs to be instantly accessible, but at the same time store out of the way when not in use. It also has to be solid. I also prefer a bipod to be

Monopods are a great option for the walking hunter in diverse terrain, as they can easily be adapted from every position from sitting to offhand.

adjustable for elevation (from prone through sitting) as well as have leveling capabilities. The last requirement is almost a necessity. If a bipod doesn't have tilt leveling, it makes actual field use very difficult. I've used models with a panning function as well, but it's been my experience that in order to have a bipod pan horizontally, much is sacrificed in the way of stability. I prefer to simply move the bipod if a target is moving across my shooting lane.

Monopods

Recently there has been a resurgence of monopods afield and, while they're not as steady as bipods, they're versatile and work in terrain where a bipod will not. For example, if your hunting area is covered in sagebrush flats, and kneeling is the only position that allows good enough visibility for a shot, a monopod can suffice. I've been using the Stoney Point monopod. It's adjustable from a sitting elevation all the way up to standing, and it has a v-notch on top for added stability. The bottom features a rubber foot with a steel spike so it can be used on a variety of terrain, from mud to solid rock to ice, and still remain stable. For certain applications, it is hard to beat.

Shooting Sticks

Shooting sticks are possibly the oldest form of rifle supports and were commonly used by the buffalo hunters of the American West. Traditionally, they were simply two sticks approximately 3 feet long and lashed together with

rawhide roughly 4 to 6 inches from the top. When the sticks were separated, they formed a "V" on top that cradled the rifle's forearm.

Now, 150 years later, shooting sticks are back, and the design has remained pretty much the same. However, some modern technology has been incorporated to make shooting sticks more lightweight and easier to use.

Most shooting sticks today are made from high-strength aluminum tubing. Some are shock-corded together, much like common tent poles, while others have a tension-adjustment nut for the different sections. Instead of being lashed together with rawhide, they now feature some sort of rubber or plastic cup that holds the two poles together as well as cradles the rifle.

Shooting sticks are not as stable or as convenient to use as a traditional bipod, but they do have the advantage of almost infinite adjustment. For diverse terrain, they may be just the ticket.

*   *   *

Predators can be hunted with a wide variety of guns and accessories. I've taken coyotes with guns from the newly introduced .17 HMR up to and including the .375 H&H. The .17s, both centerfire and rimfire, are fun and great for varmints and crows. They work well for predators within favorable range and wind conditions, but I consider them a little on the light side as an overall pred-

Shooting sticks are another good option for the roving hunter. Many models are lightweight and can be collapsed to carry in a belt holster.

ator rifle, primarily from the standpoint of versatility and wind drift. Anything like the .270 and larger is probably overkill for coyote-sized game. Good choices can be described as follows.

For hunting coyotes, foxes and bobcats in relatively open country, I would pick a bolt-action rifle chambered for a standard factory-available cartridge in the .22 to .25 caliber range that carries a bullet between 50 and 100 grains somewhere over 3,000 fps. This will provide enough energy to make clean kills and a flat enough trajectory to cover the required distances. Top it off with a good-quality variable scope in the 4x-14x range. To maximize accuracy and consequently the range of the rifle, I would add a swiveling bipod.

For chase-hunting bears or cougars, a lightweight saddle carbine using a cartridge heavy enough to do the job (something over 1,000 foot-pounds of energy) would be hard to beat. When hunting bears in heavy cover, I want a gun that hits hard enough to stop them quick: from a .300 Win Mag on up.

Any shotgun suitable for geese or turkeys loaded with large shot (BB or larger) should be adequate for coyote-sized predators.

Shiny bluing and polished wood stocks tend to reflect light and can alert a predator to your position. Covering a gun up with paint, tape or a sock is a good idea.

11
Cartridge and Bullet Selection

After calling for what seemed like an eternity, I finally got a glimpse of the coyote. He paused cautiously on the distant rise, surveying the area. A few more mouse squeaks convinced him to investigate further. Slowly trotting over the ridge, he headed in my direction. He was only about 200 yards away, but the rifle I held in my hands was not suited for even this meager distance. The coyote disappeared into a small swale between us. When he appeared again, he was 100 yards away and facing me.

I centered the fine dot of the scope on his chest, and waited. A hundred yards was still a long way for this rifle, and I didn't want to take a marginal shot. Suddenly the coyote looked back over his shoulder, in the direction he'd come, exposing his left flank and ribs. I shifted the dot to this vital area and squeezed the trigger. At the diminutive crack of the .17 HMR, the coyote jumped, spun around in circles, recovered and took off on a dead run. He only ran a short distance before collapsing.

From the tiny .17 Remington to Nitro Express elephant guns, coyotes have been taken with calibers of both extremes of the spectrum and probably everything in between at one time or another. Following is a run-down of some of the more suitable predator cartridges, as well as some of the best for certain species:

Author with a coyote he killed with a .17 HMR. While the cartridge did the job, it is not enough medicine to really be considered a "coyote" caliber.

The Small Bores

"Small bore" is a relative term. When used in a discussion on African dangerous-game hunting, it generally means to anything smaller than .375 H&H. To many hunters in North America, however, it implies any caliber with less energy than a .22 centerfire cartridge. For small predator hunting, I feel there are really only four that make the cut: the .22 Long Rifle, the .22 Winchester Magnum, the new .17 HMR and the .17 Remington.

The .22 Winchester Magnum is a significant step up from the .22 LR, and it can be used on coyotes, foxes and bobcats if the range is kept short. One nice thing about this cartridge is the lack of pelt damage it does on thin-skinned animals like foxes.

The Venerable .22 Long Rifle

The common .22 LR has probably accounted for more small predators than most other calibers combined — not because it's the most effective cartridge, but because it's undoubtedly the most common. Billions of .22 rounds are shot each year, and more than a few are launched at predators.

A 32- to 40-grain "heeled" lead bullet is propelled anywhere from 1,000 feet per second to over 1,600 fps, depending upon the load. While it's extremely accurate and is a mainstay of Olympic competition, it should only be used on fox-sized game at close range.

As a true general predator cartridge, the .22 LR is extremely lacking in bullet performance and power. It's adequate for foxes, with a rapidly expanding bullet, but nothing more. I've shot some coyotes with it using high-velocity expanding bullets such as the CCI Stinger, and only recovered about half of them. The ones I did recover were shot at less then 50 yards and hit in the heart/lungs – and they still traveled some distance before expiring. Typically, unless struck in the head or spine, most coyotes I've seen shot with a .22 LR would jump at the hit, spin around and head for parts unknown. Even with a fatal shot, it takes a while for a .22 LR to kill a coyote, and should probably be passed up for heavier loads that are capable of a more humane death.

More .22 LRs are shot every year than any other cartridge. With a rapidly expanding bullet, it can be used for foxes at close range, but it should not be considered a predator round.

The recently introduced .17 HMR is a necked-down .22 WMR loaded with a 17-grain polymer-tipped .17 caliber bullet. Velocity is impressive, and it will work well on close-range foxes, but for animals any larger, a hunter should step up to a centerfire caliber.

The .17 Remington is a completely different category than the .17 HMR. This hot little number pushes a 25-grain pill at over 4,000 fps. Where wind is not a concern, it will work for foxes, coyotes and bobcats.

A Step Up – The .22 Winchester Magnum Rimfire

The .22 WMR is to the .22 LR what a bobcat is to a housecat. There's simply no comparison. The velocity is over 2,200 fps in many loads with a jacketed bullet designed to expand rapidly for maximum energy transfer. The .22 Magnum has roughly twice the energy of any of the .22 LRs. While not a long-range varmint cartridge, it's powerful enough for foxes and coyotes out to 100 yards. I've shot several coyotes with the .22 WMR, and the results have been very satisfying. Out to 100 yards, the .22 Magnum is extremely effective and causes little pelt damage.

The .17 HMR

New in 2002, this cartridge really turned some heads as the first rimfire cartridge to come along since the ill-fated 5mm Remington introduced in 1970. New is always interesting, but what kept people looking were the ballistic numbers. This little cartridge is serious medicine for fox and limited coyote shooting.

The polymer-tipped V-Max 17-grain slug leaves the muzzle at roughly 2,550 fps. The boattail design of the diminutive bullet creates a ballistic coefficient of .125, which helps retain velocity and energy much better than any of the rimfire .22s.

If a .22 LR is to be used for coyotes, select hypervelocity ammo (over 1,500 fps) with good, rapidly expanding bullets. Keep your shots under 50 yards and be absolutely sure of your bullet placement.

One big advantage to the various centerfire .22s is the large selection of bullets available.

The .243 Winchester is considered by many to be the ideal mid-caliber predator cartridge. When combined with an accurate rifle such as the Weatherby Super Predator Master, it makes for a perfect predator combination.

While wind drift can be a problem, it's a problem on any of the smaller calibers. On a calm day, this cartridge is flat-enough shooting to be a true 150-yard fox gun and a 100-yard coyote rifle.

At the time of this writing, I was using several of the new prototype .17 HMR rifles from Ruger and Marlin. I shot a couple of coyotes with the Ruger, and both expired quickly. However, shots must be limited to 100 yards or less, and broadside targets are desirable as the bullet penetrates very little.

The Wildcat That Went Legit – The .17 Remington

In the 1970s, there was a huge interest by wildcatters in .17 caliber cartridges. While many of the designs had their individual merits, only one ever got made into a commercial factory-loaded cartridge: the .17 Remington. Essentially it is a .223 case necked down to .17 caliber. This cartridge was ahead of its time and never created a huge following among the general shooting community. This was due to several factors. When it was first introduced, powders and barrels were not of the quality commonly seen today. They tended to foul rapidly with high-velocity, overbored cartridges such as the .17 Remington. In addition to the fouling problem, bullet technology was not as good as today, and many of the early .17 caliber bullets would simply "blow up" on the skin of an animal with no penetration. However, with better bullets, powders and barrels, these problems are no longer much of a concern. Like any hot cartridge, the .17 still fouls barrels, but not to the point that it severely affects accuracy, and today's bullets are more than adequate for all predators up to coyotes. Even with its early faults, the .17 Remington has always had a small cult-like following.

The .17 Remington has been available in a factory rifle from Remington and Sako for a long time. But when Remington released their 700 Classic in .17 Remington, its popularity got a big boost, and people are experimenting with it all over again.

I bought one of the 700 Classics when it was first introduced and have shot hundreds of rounds through it. I've used it to harvest 30 or so coyotes, a couple of foxes as well as countless prairie dogs and crows. This cartridge is amazing! The velocity of the factory ammunition is over 4,000 fps with a 25-grain bullet, and the trajectory is staggeringly flat. Like all small-caliber bullets, wind drift can be a problem. However, limited to calm days afield, shooting results are impressive.

Loaded with the right bullets, the .17 Remington can anchor coyote-sized predators out to 250 yards and do very little pelt damage. On the coyotes I've shot, there is usually only a tiny entrance hole and no exit wound – a perfect pelt-saving cartridge.

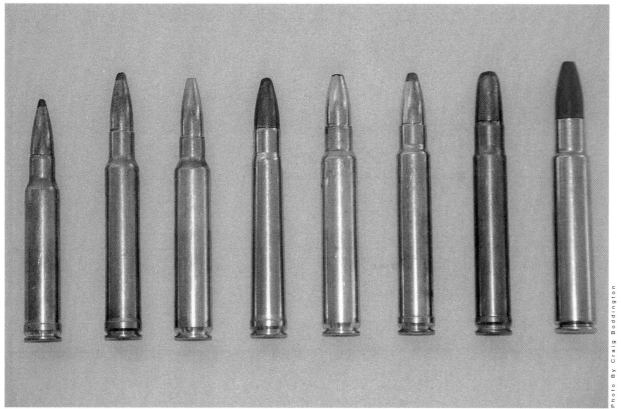

When bear hunting, you want a cartridge that's large enough to create a good blood trail and tough enough to penetrate the animal's front shoulder.

The Centerfire .22s

This group as a whole comprises the bulk of today's predator cartridges. Small-bore .22 bullets have enough weight to penetrate well, sufficient energy to anchor coyote-sized predators farther than any of us can consistently hit them, and enough velocity for a flat trajectory. Loaded right, they are ideal for foxes, bobcats and coyotes. A predator hunter would be hard-pressed to find a more versatile cartridge than a centerfire .22.

Here is a run down of the "big four" centerfire .22s used today. This is obviously not a complete list, just some of the more common cartridges in the group.

.222 Remington

The .222 Remington was introduced in 1950, chambered in the Remington Model 722. The timing for this cartridge was perfect, as hunters and shooters were flocking to the fields in search of predators and varmints, and a relatively new sport called "benchrest shooting" was just taking off in popularity. The flat trajectory and awesome accuracy of the .222 endeared it to both crowds, and within 10 years of being introduced, dominated both field and competitive events.

Until the arrival of the PPC cartridges in the mid-1970s, many shooters considered the .222 to be the most accurate cartridge ever made. Today, the popularity of the .222 has dwindled to a fraction of what it was a generation ago. As previously stated, the PPC line of cartridges dominates the benchrest circuit, and most varmint/predator hunters use the .223 Remington, as it is more common and has slightly better ballistics than the .222 (when compared bullet to bullet, the .223 is roughly 300 fps faster than a .222). But for those who enjoy hunting with a classic predator cartridge, the .222 can bring home the pelts as well as it once did.

.223 Remington

During the mid 1950s, three .22 centerfire cartridges were in contention to become our next military cartridge: the .222 Winchester, .224 Springfield and the .222 Special. When the dust settled, the .222 Special won out and was soon renamed the .223 Remington.

Today, the .223 (5.56 x 45mm) is still heavily used by armies around the world and has become the most popular .22 centerfire among civilian shooters. The reason for the popularity is obvious to anyone who has done much experimenting with this classic cartridge. It digests a large variety of bullets well, and at 3,700 fps, it shoots flat enough to be considered a 300-yard predator cartridge. In addition to the high velocity and large selection of bullets, it has a mild report, little recoil and is easy on barrels. All and all, the .223 Remington is an ideal predator caliber for most predator hunting tasks.

.220 Swift

Introduced in 1935 by Winchester, the .220 Swift is considered by many to be the best long-range predator cartridge in the world. The .220 Swift is currently the fastest .22 centerfire cartridge that's commercially available. Norma of Sweden lists the 220 Swift with a 50-grain bullet at 4,110 fps.

While it does have its proponents, since its inception it has battled rumor after rumor about its "poor performance" by naysayers. Complaints have included bullets disintegrating in midair, barrel-fouling difficulties, barrel burnout and poor accuracy. While some of these rumors may have been true 50 years ago, today they don't hold much water. Modern barrel steel, smoother cut rifling, better bullets and cleaner powders all contribute to a cartridge that is capable of producing some phenomenal groups and an acceptable level of fouling. "Burned-out" barrels are likewise a thing of the past. It is known that higher-velocity cartridges (especially those over 3,500 fps) will significantly decrease a barrel's life. For the average predator hunter, however, this should not be too much of a concern, as most barrels will outlive their owners by a comfortable margin.

.22-250 Remington

Many consider the .22-250 to be one of the most flexible and useful long-range .22s for predator hunting. While not quite as hot as the .220 Swift, it is more than adequate for all predators up to mountain lions and can be considered a true 400-yard cartridge. What it lacks in speed (when compared to the Swift), it makes up for in popularity and is a close second to the venerable .223 with dozens of factory loadings available (something that cannot be said of the Swift).

The .22-250 has been around in a wildcat form as long as the Swift, but it wasn't until 1965 that Remington decided to legitimize it as a factory cartridge. In recent years, manufacturers have been experimenting with lighter bullets to achieve higher velocities, and while everyone has their own opinion on what bullet constitute the best all-around predator medicine, it's hard to argue with the some of the current lightweight offerings that are breaking the 4,000 fps barrier.

The Mid-Calibers

In the mid-caliber selection, I include such cartridges as .243, .25-06, 6mm, .270 and 7mm-08. A great virtue of these calibers is that, aside from their effectiveness for predators, they also make a good

Bullets are designed for different functions, and they don't perform the same. In some situations, complete disintegration is desirable, while other times complete weight retention is the goal. The bottom line: Match the bullet to your intended target and hunting situation.

general rifle for deer, antelope and other medium-sized game, effectively filling a dual role.

These are the "jack-of-all-trades" predator calibers. They're not limited to any one particular type of hunting, but are adequate for a variety of game. While they may be a bit much for coyotes, I've found they don't really do much more damage to a pelt than an exploding .22 centerfire bullet (in some cases quite a bit less).

Next to being versatile, wind resistance is their big advantage over lesser calibers. Predator hunting, especially for coyotes and foxes, often takes place on the open, wind-swept plains. After reviewing a drop chart and wind-drift table, it's easy to see that wind drift plays as much a part on long-range shooting success as trajectory. The bullet's heavier weight, combined with a high ballistic coefficient, make for a noticeable advantage when the wind starts to howl.

Bores for Bears

Bruins require their own brand of medicine, as my first encounter with a large black bear proved only too well. I was hunting over a small overgrown apple orchard in western Washington, where a relatively large blackie had been spotted. The sun was dipping lower on the horizon and filtering through the trees, painting the ground in a palette of shades and colors. I'd been there since midafternoon, but knew the last few minutes of light would be the most critical for success.

Since the shooting in this brush-choked evergreen jungle was sure to be close, I had what I thought was an appropriate arm: a .308 Remington 760 semiauto Woods Master with a low-power scope. From everything I had

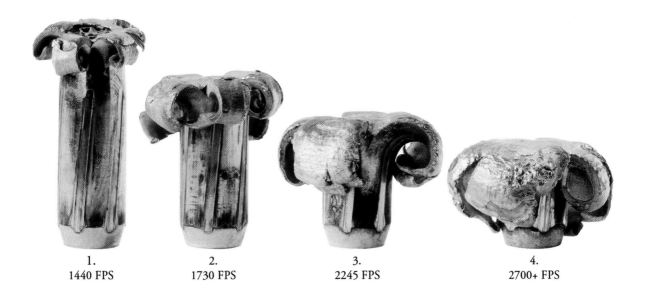

1.	2.	3.	4.
1440 FPS	1730 FPS	2245 FPS	2700+ FPS

Premium controlled-expansion bullets should expand dependably over a wide range of velocities, and maintain a high jacket core integrity.

read, the gun was sure to be enough for bear. Coincidentally, I also had my .45 auto that I often carried in the woods.

Looking at my watch, I realized time had slipped by and only a few minutes of legal shooting light remained. I was about ready to pack up and try again another night when I heard an almost inaudible crack of a breaking twig. Through the gloom and dense brush, I saw the dark outline of a bear 25 yards away. I steadied my rifle over my knee, and waited. The bear took a couple more cautious steps into the open orchard.

He turned broadside at 20 yards. I centered the crosshairs on the soft spot right behind his elbow and squeezed the trigger. The shot broke the evening calm. The bear's legs crumpled beneath him, and he hit the dirt like a sack of potatoes. It was the same reaction I'd seen from deer and didn't give it a second thought – I knew the bear was dead.

But the bear didn't know it. He bounced up like a rubber ball and was instantly on the run. More alarming, he was running full-tilt directly toward me!

I centered the cross hairs and shot again. This time there was no reaction at all. Thankful for having a semi-auto, I squeezed the trigger for a third shot. When nothing happened, I looked down and sure enough, there was a spent cartridge "stove piped" and protruding out of the half-closed action. I was no longer thankful for the semi-auto.

I dropped the rifle and grabbed my pistol as the bear closed within 10 yards. I aimed for his head as he came

straight at me and fired two shots. There was no effect – not even a flinch. At five paces, I decided I didn't want to be bowled over by a running bear and stood up, pistol still in hand. Upon seeing me, the bear turned broadside and I fired two more shots at his chest. He wheeled and ran back the way he'd come, and I fired two more shots at his fleeing rump (a shot I'd never take on an unwounded animal).

I heard him crash through the brush as the daylight slipped away. It was over in a few seconds, but seemed like hours at the time. Considerably shaken, I sat down against the base of a tree and wondered what the heck had just happened. I knew I'd hit him hard with the first and second shots. I wasn't sure about the pistol, as there was absolutely no reaction. A cursory look in the growing darkness showed no dead bear or obvious blood trail. Since it was early fall and the sun would be up before 5 a.m., I decided to return in the morning to start tracking him.

Looking over the scene at first light, I found a few dabs of blood where the bear had first hit the ground, then no more. I trailed him to the path in the woods where he disappeared and found another drop of blood. Two hundred yards away, through the heaviest cover, I found the dead bear. The entire "blood trail" would not have filled a shot glass. As for the bullets, the evidence was all there. Two .308 slugs penetrated the chest and exited with minimal tissue damage. The pistol shots were all accounted for and had inflicted some wounds that would have eventually killed the bear, but a .45 is too light for this work. The animal's heavy fur had soaked up a lot of blood, but

Partition-style bullets incorporate a divider between the front and the rear core, thereby limiting expansion so penetration is ensured.

the wounds had clogged with fat and did not leak enough blood to make an effective trail.

I learned on that day, when hunting bears, you want a cartridge that's large enough to create a good blood trail and also tough enough to penetrate the front shoulder. That's where you want to shoot a bear, not in the heart. Break the front shoulder and the animal won't travel far.

For black bears, I only use premium bullets. I use my Sako .375 H&H as well. Do I need this much rifle? In open cover, for Lower 48 bears that often weigh less than 250 pounds, probably not. But for larger bears in heavy cover, I can attest it's not overkill. While a large-caliber rifle sometimes may be needed, any of the high-powered .30s will work fine, provided you select the right bullet for the job. The .308, .30-06, .300 Win Mag and .338 are all good picks for bears, with a tendency toward the .300 Win Mag if your hunt may also involve shooting across canyons and large openings where a flat trajectory is useful.

Not All Bullets Are Created Equal

Bullet performance seems to be one of the least-understood aspects of hunting. Bullets come in many shapes and sizes, designed to perform differently under various conditions. Without getting bogged down in a bunch of technical terms and jargon that few shooters need or want to know, enough of the basics can be discussed to help the average hunter select a bullet suitable for his use.

The two primary bullet characteristics of concern to the hunter are deformation of the slug on impact and retention of energy during flight. These are somewhat interrelated, but can be discussed separately.

The degree of deformation, commonly referred to as "expansion," is determined by bullet material, design structure and velocity at impact. Bullets can be roughly categorized as "minimum expansion," "controlled expansion" and "premium controlled expansion."

Minimum-expansion bullets tend to punch a small hole and penetrate deeply. A solid soft lead slug from a .22 rimfire traveling at relatively low speed expands very little, and is a good example of this. Most handgun ammunition falls in this category. Military ammunition is made to penetrate but not cause excessive tissue damage. Big solid or fully jacketed bullets are meant to punch through tough hide, bone and flesh into the vitals of large and dangerous African game.

Controlled-expansion bullets incorporate some means to achieve a desired degree of deformation. A hollow point on a .22 Long Rifle bullet is an example. The desired degree of deformation depends on the planned usage. A light, fragile bullet at very high velocity that literally explodes on impact might be desirable for prairie dogs and crows. A heavier slug with a tapered metal jacket and exposed soft point that makes a uniform mushroom but stays in one piece is better for larger game. Such bullets perform best at an optimum range (i.e. impact velocity). At close range or impact on a heavy bone, they may break apart and not penetrate deeply enough. At extended range, they may fail to deform properly.

Premium controlled-expansion bullets incorporate additional refinements of design and construction that widen the optimum range and tend to compensate for margins of error. These features are intended to prevent the slug from breaking apart, thus retaining a good portion intact to penetrate adequately. Various techniques are used, such as partitioned jackets, ringed jackets, bonded cores, solid bases, steel inserts, etc. Premium bullets may also use further refinements such as moly coatings and boat tail shapes to reduce barrel friction and fouling and improve flight characteristics. Some examples of premium bullets include Nosler Partition Gold, Swift A-frames, Barnes X, Trophy Bonded Bear Claw and Hornady Interlocs.

Retention of energy during flight is basically determined by bullet weight and shape. Just as light birdshot slows faster than heavy shot, a light bullet loses energy faster than a heavy bullet started at the same speed. Similarly, a long streamlined bullet retains energy (i.e. velocity) longer than a short blunt one of the same weight. The technical term is "ballistic coefficient" and that's about all you need to know about it. Retention of energy is important to the hunter because it strongly influences effective range, accuracy, energy at impact, drop and wind drift.

How can you use all this information? Consider the size of the animal being hunted, the ranges and terrain where you hunt, external factors such as wind, then study ballistic tables and select good-quality cartridges and bullets adequate for the job.

12

Choosing and Using Optics

The technology for enhancing human vision with various combinations of glass lenses, mirrors and prisms has been around since the invention of the telescope some 400 years ago. In the last few generations, fantastic advances in the field of optics and associated electronics have been made. Modern versions of sights, binoculars, night scopes and other devices provide capabilities that would have been unbelievable just a few years ago. Manufacturers offer an enormous range of products, from the most basic to the highly sophisticated, at a price spread to fit any budget.

Not every hunter needs or can afford the most elaborate optical devices. You can certainly have a lot of fun – and be reasonably successful – hunting predators with the basic gear. Some of the same items you use to hunt larger game or shoot varmints are also suitable for predator hunting. However, it's good to understand the advanced optical items that are available and the reasons quality costs more … and why it may be worth the price.

Telescopic Sights

The Germans have been designing and tinkering with riflescopes for over 150 years, but it wasn't until after World War II that modern telescopic rifle sights became an affordable option for most American hunters.

One of the first commercially available scopes on the American scene was the venerable Weaver Alaskan series. This quickly became popular among hunters, but it wasn't long until there were several others to choose from. Today, there are dozens of scope manufacturers, each offering several models. It's no wonder hunters have a hard time choosing the right scope for their needs. Here are some things to consider when selecting a scope for predator hunting.

Binoculars can be as important to a predator hunter as a rifle.

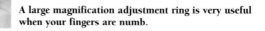

Magnification on a riflescope can either be fixed or adjustable, as in the case of this Leupold Vari-X III.

A large magnification adjustment ring is very useful when your fingers are numb.

Optics for predator hunting are almost as important as the rifle itself.

Author using a variable Leupold scope. When calling, keep the power turned down in case of a surprise appearance of a predator, but be ready to crank it up if a long shot presents itself.

Magnification

How much magnification you'll need depends on the type of predator you're seeking, the terrain you're hunting and the method you're using. This doesn't mean you'll need a different scope for each type of hunting. It simply means that you ought to consider certain factors before making a purchase. No single scope, like no single rifle, is perfect for all situations, but you can select one that does many things well.

Don't buy more scope than you need. Many novice hunters have the notion that predator hunting is a long-range affair, so high-powered scopes are a must. Nothing could be further from the truth. Most predators are taken at relatively short distances, usually less than 150 yards. I've probably shot as many coyotes within 25 yards as I have beyond 300 yards.

For this reason, I prefer high-quality, adjustable-power scopes with a low-end magnification of around 4x and a top end of around 14x. I feel that this variable range covers most situations pretty well.

When I get to a stand and start calling, I make sure the scope is cranked down to its lowest setting. Too many times I've had a coyote run right in, dodging and weaving through the sagebrush, only to shoulder my rifle and not find the animal because the power was cranked all the way up. Keeping the power on the lowest setting will keep you ready for those close shots. Almost always, you'll have plenty of time to crank the power up for the longer shots.

There once was an argument for fixed-power scopes. Variables were not as reliable and cost more than their fixed-power counterparts. That's no longer the case. Modern variable scopes are every bit as clear, shockproof, waterproof and fogproof as fixed-power scopes. Variables are also available at about the same price.

A good all-around scope for predators such as coyotes, foxes and bobcats where calling is the main method of hunting, is a variable scope in the 4x-14x category. If most calling is to be in brushy or timbered country, I might pick something on the lower end of this scale, such as a 2x or 3x low end and a 10x high end. The classic 3x-9x works perfectly for this type of hunting. If most hunting is to be done out on the plains or other extremely open country where longer shots are a more frequent opportunity, I opt for a scope with a little more power, say a 6x-18x or 6x-20x.

More often than not, bears and cougars are shot fairly close. Because the animals are large and the light is poor in the dense cover where they are usually found, I pick a scope that has a very low end with good light-gathering capabilities, such as a 1.5x-6x. I currently have such a scope made by Swarovski on my bear rifle and like it very much. For close encounters in thick cover, the super-large field of view and great light gathering provided by the 1.5x setting make it ideal. And if a shot across a clear-cut presents itself, the 6x magnification makes it possible.

Objective lenses come in different sizes, but size alone is not the only measurement of a scope's quality.

The more optical coatings there are on a riflescope, binoculars or spotting scope, the better.

Size Does Matter (Sometimes)

Objective lens size seems to be the rage in today's scope-marketing campaigns. Expressed in millimeters (such as 40mm, 44mm and 50mm), the diameter of the front lens (the objective lens) does play a part in how well the scope gathers light, but it's not everything.

Based on the theory that bigger is better, consumers today are buying more 50mm scopes than ever before. Why? Because they believe those scopes gather more light and therefore perform better under low-light conditions. This seems to make sense on the surface, but doesn't tell the whole story.

Light-gathering ability is determined by several factors. Objective lens size is only one. Optical quality is another. Internal design and overall optical quality are still others. For example, you can have the largest objective lens in the world, but if it's made from glass with poor light transmitting capability, it won't gather light nearly as well as a multicoated, hi-tech piece half its size.

The same applies to internal construction and design. Some scope manufacturers, trying to ride the large-objective lens craze, have simply enlarged the front-end glass of their products. Aside from making the scope large and bulky, it does little to improve low-light performance. The quality of the glass inside the tube must also be enhanced. This is why larger 30mm main tubes are so common on high-end optics. Sometimes 30mm main tubes are used for looks or to add windage and elevation adjustment, so tube size alone can't be relied upon as an indication of performance.

I've used several high-quality German optics with comparatively small objective lenses, but were brighter under low-light conditions than larger but cheaper scopes. So yes, there can be a substantial light-gathering gain by going to a larger-objective lens, but at the same time, the overall design and quality of the device is also very important. This is truly a case of "you get what you pay for."

As a general rule, all other factors being equal, the lower the magnification power and the larger the external and internal optics, the better the scope will perform when the light fades.

Optical Coatings

There's more than meets the eye to manufacturers' claims on anti-reflective coatings. You may wonder why coatings are needed to begin with. It's really simple. Uncoated glass can reflect up to 5 percent of the light transmitted through it. Considering that a set of optics may contain as many as 10 glass surfaces, it's easy to see that nearly half of the available light may be lost. Much of that light stays inside the device, where it bounces around and causes glare and diminished contrast.

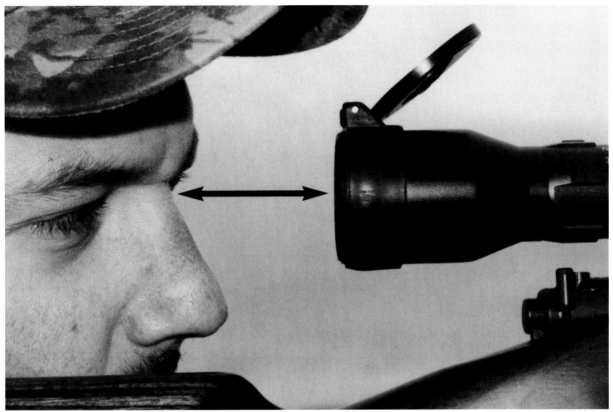
Eye relief is the distance from the ocular lens that the viewer can comfortably obtain a full field of view.

Coatings are chemical films (commonly magnesium fluoride) applied to the surface of the glass. While a single coating is good, more are better. Here's a breakdown of the terms used to describe the different levels of coating.

Coated Optics – one or more glass surfaces on at least one lens have received an anti-reflective optical coating.

Fully Coated – all glass surfaces have been coated with an anti-reflective optical coating.

Multicoated – one or more glass surfaces on at least one lens have received multiple anti-reflective optical coatings.

Fully Multicoated – all glass surfaces have received multiple anti-reflective optical coatings.

It's easy to misunderstand and be misled by these terms. For example, if a manufacturer puts two coats on one single lens, he can claim to have multicoated optics. This is where cost of the finished product may vary. The top manufacturers multicoat all glass surfaces within their optics. Since this takes time, precision and materials, it costs more, but the final product is much sharper and performs better in low light.

Field of View

Field of View is a measurement of the sight picture expressed in feet at 100 yards (sometimes 1,000 yards) and can be used as a comparison between scopes. I prefer as wide a field of view as possible for any given power setting. Predators are often shot on the move, and a larger field of view helps in acquiring targets. Magnification has an inverse relationship with field of view – the higher the power, the narrower the field of view.

Eye Relief

Eye Relief is the distance from the ocular (rear) lens of the scope to your eye while maintaining a full image. Usually expressed as a range, this distance varies from scope to scope, and in the case of a variable scope, varies with power. Generous eye relief is not as critical in predator hunting as it is in big-game hunting. One of the main advantages of lots of eye relief is the ability to keep your face farther away from the scope – important when you're using a hard-recoiling rifle. Since lighter-kicking firearms are more of the norm when chasing predators, eye relief is not as important as other scope factors.

For use on a handgun, you'll need a specially designed scope with an eye relief of 12 to 24 inches. This will allow you to hold the gun in a normal shooting position and still see the full image.

Reticles

It's not a simple choice of light or heavy crosshairs anymore. Hunters today can choose from many different

In the West, binoculars are a critical part of a predator hunter's arsenal.

reticle options including, heavy duplex, fine duplex, target dot, fine crosshair, single post, three-post, mil-dot and multiple variations of each.

Which type is best? For most hunters, the choice will boil down to their type of hunting and personal preference. Here are a few suggestions:

For coyotes, foxes and bobcats under normal lighting condition, a standard duplex works great. The heavier lines make for easy target acquisition and the fine crosshairs allow for precise shot placement.

Some like mil-dots for long-range shooting, but I prefer the Night Force predator reticle. It has several holdover hash marks as well as a very useful rangefinding function specifically sized for coyotes.

For low-light or night hunting, heavy duplex crosshairs work OK, but a lighted reticle works even better. In either case, use the lowest power setting so the scope can transmit as much light as possible.

Lighted Reticles

The first scope I had with a lighted reticle was a Night Force long-range scope, and it sold me on illuminated reticles for predator hunting. Predators are often shot at first and last light, and even at night. Seeing black crosshairs on a dark background is difficult. A lighted reticle should not be confused with a laser sight, a HOLOsight or a night scope. It's simply a standard scope that has an LED that illuminates the crosshairs (or other type reticle) for easier viewing in low-light conditions. Most of the units are powered by a small hearing aid-type battery and have a built-in rheostat to adjust the brightness of the reticle. This brightness varies from a dull, almost unnoticeable glow to a bright red. If the battery runs out or you don't have time to turn it on, the crosshairs appear as they would on a normal scope without the lighted function.

For night hunting, this type of scope works great and is superior to other forms of lighted optics that must be turned on before the reticle is visible (with the exception of the Trijicon system, which uses a chemical that constantly glows green day or night). This means you either must leave the scope on and risk depleting the battery, or hope you have enough time and freedom of movement to turn the unit on when needed – not the best scenario for hunting applications.

Quality Versus Cost

Riflescopes generally range in price from under $50 to over $1,500. They all magnify an image, so why the big difference in price? The answer is quality. This doesn't mean you have to spend $1,500 to get a good hunting scope, but you obviously won't get top quality for $29.99. To those who have used both extremes, the difference is evident.

First, consider the glass. Glass is not just glass. Glass varies in clarity, distortion and reflection. The number and styles of coatings applied to glass provides clarity as well as good low-light performance and depth of field. The best products will have fully multi-coated optics – which means that every side of every piece of glass gets multiple coatings. Cheaper scopes may have only one external side coated; some may not have any.

In addition to glass quality, construction figures into the price. The best manufacturers use a single one-piece tube. It costs more to construct, but it is more durable, weatherproof and can withstand greater amounts of shock than multiple-piece tubes.

Internal adjustments are another means of comparison. Quality scopes use precise adjustment mechanisms. This means that if you make a certain number of clicks, it will move the point of impact the correct number of inches at the given distance. Conversely, if you go back the same amount of clicks, the point of aim should return to its original setting. Like a fine watch or micrometer, this sort or precision does not come free – hence the bigger price tag. Cheaper scopes also often "bind" and then suddenly move several inches with one or two clicks. This makes sighting in a chore as well making click adjustments for long-range compensation an impossibility.

Night Vision Optics

Night vision works by collecting minute particles of light, called photons, which cannot be seen with the naked eye, and focusing them into an image intensifier. This collects the photons and converts them to electrons, which are then multiplied thousands of times and projected onto a green phosphorescent screen. When this intensified electron image strikes the screen, it causes the screen to emit light that is visible to the naked eye. It's this phosphorus screen that gives the characteristic green glow to night vision scenes.

The whole process is complex, but night vision essentially works like a radio amplifier, taking small electrical charges not detectable to the human senses and multiplying them to a level that we can use.

While the entire process is complex, all we need to know is what separates the lower-priced units from the very expensive. The differences are really quite easy to understand. Night vision optics have been around since World War II and have gone through many improvements, called generations (GEN). With each generation, the end picture quality, range and light-gathering ability improve. It's these differences, combined with the overall size, weight and technical features, that dictate the price. Here is a rundown of the different generations available to the public.

Rangefinders are a useful tool. The new laser rangefinders are small, lightweight and extremely accurate. In recent years, they have also dropped significantly in price.

First-Generation Night Optics

GEN I optics were developed in the 1960s and are still the most widely used night vision optics used today. They need some visible light to operate and do not function well in extremely dark environments. But for general night use with the aid of stars and moonlight, combined with extra infrared illumination, they work well enough for most applications. The biggest advantage to GEN I optics is definitely price. GEN I monoculars can be had for a quarter of what some of the GEN II and GEN III models cost.

Second-Generation Night Optics

GEN II optics were developed in the 1970s. They have a significantly longer lifespan and do not require visible light to operate, which allows them to work in extremely dark conditions. They also offer a clearer picture/resolution than GEN I optics and are a good choice for night optics when details (such as hunting applications) need to be seen.

Third-Generation Night Optics

GEN III optics have been developed in recent years and are currently the state of the art in night vision. GEN III optics have a greatly increased amount of light-gaining ability and resolution (clarity) over both GEN I and II optics. They're the ideal choice for discriminating night vision enthusiasts, law enforcement and military personnel. For night hunting applications, they also work extremely well, offering excellent detail and range. The only disadvantage of GEN III optics is the price. For premium performance, you pay a premium price.

Binoculars

In all forms of hunting, being able to see well simply aids in the hunter's success. In addition to a quality riflescope, a good set of binoculars is a must. Many of the same principles of quality riflescope optics also hold true for binoculars. Good coated glass, combined with quality construction, are the two main features hunter should look for when choosing binoculars.

Concerning power, I prefer something in the 8x range with large enough objective lens to gather a fair amount of light. In most predator hunting (trophy bear hunting is the exception), optics are simply used to spot approaching animals, movement and large tracts of real estate. For these situations, it's hard to beat low-powered

Optics are essential for predator hunting. Binoculars, rangefinders and rifle scopes all compliment each other in their own unique way and ultimately will increase your success rate.

binoculars. I find anything higher than 8x hard to hold steady and really not needed. High-power binoculars are generally used to judge the trophy potential of an animal.

Rangefinders

Ten years ago, rangefinders were large, clunky, slow to use, difficult to operate and not very accurate. However several years ago, rangefinders using laser technology entered the market and were an instant success. Today they're pocket-sized, relatively inexpensive, instant to use and accurate to plus or minus 1 yard.

While most rangefinders have some magnifying capabilities, they're really dedicated rangefinding units,

not optical aids. However, at least two companies (Leica and Bushnell) produce combination rangefinders/binoculars, and one, (Swarovski), makes a combination rifle-scope/rangefinder.

The first thing hunters notice about rangefinders is that they all have seemingly incredible distances they can range up to. The "lowest power" unit currently ranges to a maximum of 400 yards, while some of the upper-end models accurately range out to 1,200 yards. Keep in mind, however, that these published distances are under ideal conditions against a reflective surface such as a granite slab or metal road sign. Under field conditions on a furry animal, the actual maximum distance will usually be less than half of the published number.

13

Hiding from Predators

Camo comes in many forms, from brown work clothes to high-tech military Ghillie suits.

Back when man still stalked mastodons and avoided sabertooth tigers, camouflage was an integral part of the hunt. While it's not known for sure, those early hunters likely used animal skins and charcoal to blend in with their surroundings. Native Americans often got within touching distance of white-tailed deer and elk by draping animal skins over their bodies. In Namibia, the Kung San, the most primitive and skillful hunters on earth, wouldn't dare go on a hunt without first adorning themselves with leaves and grass to stalk within a few feet of unsuspecting kudu and gemsbok.

The point is, most wild animals can see incredibly well. If you want to be successful at hunting them, you need to take a lesson from the hunters of old and blend in with your surroundings.

A good hunter can blend in with the terrain, no matter what the surroundings look like.

Matching Your Surroundings

Camouflage. It's all the same, isn't it? Military green, Realtree, Mossy Oak, Seclusion 3D … any pattern should work, right? With all of the choices available today, it's hard to figure out which is best for fooling a wary predator. Twenty years ago, the answer was much simpler. World War II and woodland patterns were about the only camo choices available. But even though there are scores of patterns to choose from today, no pattern is best for all situations.

Those who've seen a modern hardwood camouflage pattern from a distance, especially while hunting in the open country of the West, know that it doesn't look like an oak tree, a pile of leaves or something that belongs in that landscape. What it appears to be is a large, dark, human-shaped blob. The problem is that most hardwoods patterns designed for turkey and whitetail hunters are "closed" patterns – printed on a dark background with lots of fine detail. Most blend in perfectly at 50 yards in heavy cover, but appear as a solid, dark color at longer ranges in sparse cover. Open patterns, on the other hand, are printed on a light background, blend in extremely well at longer ranges, but are not quite as effective when blending in with green, lush vegetation.

For shotgun hunting coyotes, foxes and bobcats in heavy cover, a standard hardwoods pattern should be perfect. However, for hunting in the open country of the West, some better choices are available.

That being said, I don't mean to imply that you can't call predators in close without the best camo. I've done it many times while wearing hardwoods patterns, khakis and even blue jeans. The key is to know what you can and can't get away with and matching your surroundings to compensate.

For example, if you're wearing a dark pattern in the middle of a sage-covered desert, find a small brush-choked gully or fence line to break up your outline. Sometimes shaded outcroppings or green plants such as yuccas can be used for concealment. However, don't just plop down in an open field while wearing any old pattern and expect to disappear because you're wearing some kind of camo. If I'm wearing a pattern I know blends well in open country, I don't hesitate to sit on an open hillside while calling. Still, I keep below the crest of the hill and in the shade when possible.

As mentioned, no single camo pattern works equally well under all conditions. If you hunt in different terrain types, you may need several outfits, depending upon the extent of your hunting.

Sagebrush/Desert

Open patterns are the only way to go if you want to hunt in the desert. One of the best things to come out of Operation Desert Storm, from a predator

Open patterns work well out West on the sage-covered plains.

If hunting in evergreen forests, be sure to wear a green pattern and pick a stand with enough natural foliage to help break up your outline.

hunter's perspective, was the military desert camouflage. An open pattern that looks great from a distance, it's ideal for a variety of desert landscapes. Unfortunately, most lines of clothing available in this pattern are military surplus, which are simply cotton, non-insulated and non-waterproof. Such clothing is good for warm-season hunting, but does not offer adequate protection in inclement or cold weather commonly experienced while predator hunting.

Prairie Ghost camouflage is a relatively new pattern that practically disappears in desert landscapes. The design is real-looking sagebrush tops on a light background. I've hunted predators in this camo and think it's a cut above the competition. It's available in a variety of materials for use in wet, cold or warm weather.

I've also worn Everywear West and Faded Sage camouflage. Both use the same photoprint technology as Prairie Ghost, and both look great. If you do most of your predator hunting in sagebrush or open grasslands, either of these patterns will work fine.

Thousands of ranchers across the West can attest to another type of effective camo, the standard khaki colored Carhartt clothing. While this material is a solid color, once it becomes faded and stained by dirt and a few grease spots, it makes for excellent "camo," rivaling some of the best-designed patterns.

Evergreen and Hardwood Forests

Luckily for predator hunters who hunt in the timber, most hardwoods patterns will work fine. If I'm hunting in the Midwest, I prefer more browns over greens (such as Realtree X-Tra Brown and Mossy Oak Break-Up), but if I'm hunting in an evergreen forest with lots of foliage in the underbrush, I choose a pattern like Advantage Timber.

All-Around Camo

The new Seclusion 3D from Cabela's is an extremely versatile pattern using "Optical Prioritization." The pattern creates a "chameleon" effect, making it appear green in green surroundings, brown in brown surroundings and gray in gray surroundings. This pattern is as effective at 500 yards as it is at 50 yards. It's available in many materials and in insulated and non-insulated versions, so there is something for 100-degree days as well as for the dead of winter.

Hiding in Snow

It doesn't matter what camo you choose, when the snow starts to fly, if you aren't dressed in white, you won't blend in. If you're hunting in timber, broken, rocky country or sage, you can sometimes get away with standard

Some patterns, like Seclusion 3D, are extremely versatile and work in a variety of conditions.

While white coveralls work great in a heavy snow, white snow camo breaks up the human outline even more.

Even if snow is covering the ground, regular camo will work fine if there's enough natural cover to conceal you.

While Ghillie suits do a great job of concealing hunters, there are more comfortable options available, such as this 3D leafy suit from Robinson Labs.

clothing (as some of the pictures in this book attest), but if you're caught out in barren stubble fields or winter wheat covered in snow, you're just that – caught. Only snow camo will do the trick of fooling a predator's eyes at such times.

I like the Snow Shadow Coveralls from Cabela's. It has enough of a mottled design to blend with a variety of winter settings. The one-piece extreme-weather suit is durable and is easy to remove when getting in and out of the truck or going into town. It's also the warmest suit I've used. It has kept me warm for extended calling sessions in minus 15-degree weather with a 20-mph wind.

In addition to the suit, I wear a white stocking cap and white gloves, not only for concealment, but also for warmth. Winter calling usually means frigid calling over most of my hunting area.

Add Depth to Your Disguise

So far we've concentrated on two-dimensional camo. What happens when you add a third dimension, depth? You simply vanish, as anyone who has seen 3D camo in use can attest. Many movies have depicted military snipers and other elite troops wearing such getups to remain hidden within feet of an enemy. Does it really work that well? The short answer is yes, if done correctly. However, for predator hunters, it's not a magic cure for

poor setups, ignoring wind direction or getting caught while walking to a stand. It does allow selecting a calling position where ground cover is sparse and provides a whole lot more freedom of movement should you need to change position to make a shot.

There are essentially two varieties of 3D camo. The first is the tried-and-true Ghillie Suit, developed by military snipers by tying and sewing strips of torn burlap onto a standard set of BDUs (battle dress uniform). Refined during the Vietnam War, it probably still provides the best concealment of any camo available today.

Commercially offered by several different manufacturers for hunting applications, the Ghillie suit has evolved to better fit hunters' needs. My only complaints with the suit are lack of mobility (try walking a mile to stand in one in warm temperatures, and you'll see for yourself), scent control and weatherproofness. While weatherproofness and scent control are still valid complaints, the mobility issue has been nearly eliminated from modern suits. Some manufacturers are now incorporating a set of backpack straps so the entire suit can be rolled up and carried, allowing the hunter to put it on once at his calling stand. Others have cut the suit down to a shawl size, eliminating over half of the size and weight while still retaining the breakup properties that made them famous.

Recently, other commercially made 3D options have hit the market. Originally designed for bowhunters, they also work great for predator hunters

Calling involves a lot of hand movement. Wary predators will notice the shine from your hands if you don't wear gloves.

The human face shines and reflects light. Covering it up with paint or a face mask is critical to a caller's success.

as well. These are a standard set of hunting togs with "leaves" made of material sewn in place. The leaves effectively break up an outline and flap in the slightest breeze, making the entire suit look like a giant bush. One aspect I like of the cut leaf 3D camo over standard Ghillie suits is that it's available with scent-suppressant linings as well as being bonded to a breathable membrane for protection from the elements. Since these suits do not have "leaves" inside the leges, they are much easier to walk in and lighter than old Ghillie suits. Cut-leaf camo is offered by several companies, but my favorite is 3D Realleaf by Robinson Laboratories.

Recently I tried another product called Sneaky Leaf, which are essentially fake leaves with plastic stems that can be pinned onto clothing for a brushy effect. They were inexpensive, worked incredibly well and held up throughout the season. I learned that the entire set of clothing did not have to be covered for it to be effective. a few leaves on the brim of the hat and some on the shoulders and arms were all that were needed.

Breaking up the human outline is all that's really necessary for any 3D camouflage. The oldest method of doing this is to secure natural vegetation around the brim of your hat to break up head movement and the human outline. In addition to doing this, I often position myself behind a small clump of bushes, or even pull a few branches, sticks and grass over my lap to aid in the breakup illusion.

The Little Things

The best camo on the market won't hide you from predators if you don't hide your hands and face. When you're calling, you hands are constantly moving – picking up calls, laying them down, squeezing bulb-type calls and cupping the tube of mouth calls. Predators tend to see this motion before anything else. A set of gloves is invaluable in avoiding detection. For summer wear, I like the light mesh camo gloves used by turkey hunters. In winter, I prefer Glomitts (glove/mitten combinations with a removable mitt portion). While wearing these, I can still have manual dexterity of my fingers for fine movements such as pulling the trigger and cycling the bolt of a rifle, but retain the warmth factor of a mitten.

A hunter's face rates the same attention as his hands. The human face tends to reflect light, and it's very easy for predators to see. Combined with the fact that you're constantly scanning the hills for signs of movement, it's akin to flashing a mirror back and forth and hoping a sharp-eyed predator doesn't pick up on it.

Face concealment comes in several options, from facemasks to face paint. Over the years I've used both, but now tend to stick with three-quarter masks. They are easy to remove, can be worn with a ball cap, and work well. While camo paint looks good, it's a pain to put on and remove, tends to itch when you sweat, will wear off during the course of a day's hunting and is inconvenient should you want to stop at a mini mart for a soda. Needless to say, you'll get strange looks.

Even small objects like calls can reflect light, and they should be taped to complete your disguise.

Guns and Accessories

Anything else that may reflect light or not blend in with the surroundings should also be properly camouflaged. The biggest offenders are guns, optics and calls.

Almost all of today's guns could use some "predator-izing." Stainless steel, blued metal and shiny stocks can all spook a wary predator if the sun strikes it the wrong way. There are several methods of camouflaging weapons, including spray paint, tape, slip-over socks and even factory-dip paint jobs. I've had experience with nearly every method but prefer tape and slip-over covers. Tape is nice because it can be cut to fit any application. It works especially well for covering shiny scope rings, binoculars and howling tubes. For rifles and shotguns, I like the new generation of "gun socks" made from neoprene for complete gun coverage. Not only are they easy to use and comfortable to grip, but best of all, they protect your gun from bumps and scratches.

14

In the Dark of the Night

When the sun goes down, predators often come out to play. With their built-in night vision, they have no trouble locating food.

My partner and I sneaked over the small rise and looked over the terrain. Illuminated by the whitewashed glow from the half moon, the contours and ridges could be seen even in the dark. Situated with our backs against a small outcropping of rock, I started to call.

The rabbit-in-distress cry resounding through the night air seemed too loud and out of place at such a tranquil time. After finishing a short series of calls, I looked over and motioned for my hunting partner to switch on the light.

An eerie red glow illuminated the area around us for several hundred yards. My partner panned the light from left to right, sweeping all of the available cover. Seeing nothing out of the ordinary, he turned the light off. The summer night enveloped us like a warm blanket. We sat in the dark, listening to the crickets, and waited.

After a long pause and another short calling session, he again turned on the light. Repeating his scanning pattern, he got about halfway through his search when he spotted reflection from a pair of eyes. Coyote! The twin dots were about 300 yards away – too far for a shot, especially at night. I looked through the scope, but all I could

Working the graveyard shift. Howling at night is a productive way to locate coyotes.

see were the dots – no indication of how the coyote was positioned or where to aim. Not wanting to risk making a sound by clicking the light off, Mark left the light on but pointed it slightly upward, so only the bottom edge of the beam caught the coyote's eyes. With my rifle already shouldered, I started pumping the bulb call mounted on the forearm. That was all it took. The eyes started bouncing toward our position. He was coming so fast, it looked like one of those night photos of a busy highway where all the lights blend into one, forming a moving stream of color.

I decided to let him come as close as he wanted. He showed no signs of veering from his course to sample the breeze downwind of us, nor did he have any hesitation about coming to the call.

At 40 yards, Mark shined the full light on the coyote. The light didn't spook him; he was too intent on finding the dying rabbit. Slowing down to a walk, he paused momentarily to sniff the ground at 25 yards. I centered his vitals inside of the heavy part of the duplex crosshairs and squeezed off a shot. Spinning around in circles, he went down in a cloud of dust.

That was just one of many coyotes I've called at night. The first time it happened, it was a revelation. Not only would night hunting open up more available time to hunt, but more quality opportunities as well.

Coyotes, foxes and bobcats are largely nocturnal predators. While they can be successfully called at all hours of the day, this is a bit out of character for them. Night is their true domain. In addition to normally being active at night, they also have less to fear. During the day, they get shot at by passing ranchers, they get rousted from their beds by bird hunters and, more often than not when they come to the sound of a call, hot lead greets them instead of a warm rabbit. However, at night, they rarely come into contact with people. Their preferred prey is out and about, and with their built-in night vision, they have no trouble finding it.

Timing Is Everything

Coyotes hunt at night year-round, but calling them seems to be more productive at certain times than others.

The first time I went coyote hunting after dark, the timing was just a matter of chance. A partner and I had gone on a summer coyote trip to the desert. In our youthful wisdom, we had forgot that daytime temperatures soared to well over 100 degrees there. Limited to hunting about an hour in the morning and an hour in the evening, we spent the remainder of the day lying under the shade of some sparse trees and taking dips in a small stock pond. While we felt we were wasting valuable hunting time, in retrospect I believe the coyotes were resting in the shade as well. When it turned dark and the temperature dropped to a relatively chilly 75 degrees, we headed out. Over the course of that night, we called in over a half dozen coyotes.

Predators have a hard time seeing red lights, which is why they work so well for night hunters.

Taro Sakita with one of the many coyotes he has called in at night.

Since then, I've hunted coyotes at night on numerous occasions in the summer and have always done well – in fact, better than during other times of the year. I believe this is strictly because of the heat. Coyotes aren't willing to expend the energy required to travel to a call when it's blistering hot. During colder months, it's common to see coyotes several hours after daylight and several hours before dark, and in the winter, all-day hunting is the norm. But in the summer, coyotes have no choice but to hunt at night. This means they are apt to take advantage of every opportunity, readily coming to a call.

Summer is my favorite time to night hunt, but a close second is on a calm, full-moon night in the dead of winter, after a fresh snow. Where I live, there are not many of these nights a season, but you can bet when they come, you won't find me at home. Even without a light, it's easy to see a coyote approaching a stand under these conditions, and sounds from a call carry a long way. In addition, winter coyotes travel long distances in winter, since their caloric needs are much greater than during the rest of the year. All of these factors combined make for a productive night afield.

Regardless of season, the entire night is not prime calling time. I've found that the four hours after sundown and the two hours before sunrise are the most productive. There seems to be a lull in the middle of the night when coyotes take a short siesta. This is not a proven fact, but I've witnessed it in several areas of the West.

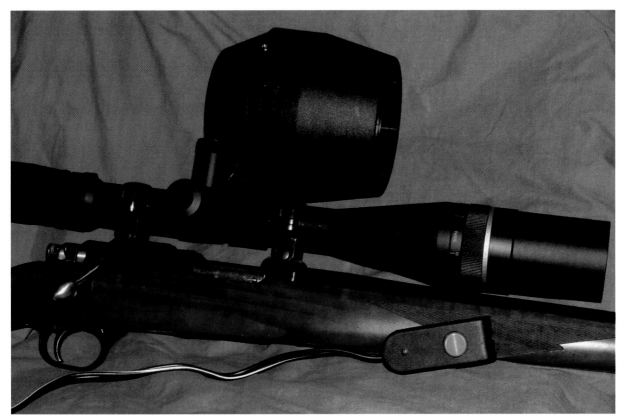

Rifle-mounted spotlights are just the ticket for nighttime predator hunting. Some models feature an on/off switch that can be mounted on a gun's forearm.

Night Hunting Equipment

Gearing up for night hunting can be as simple or as high-tech as the hunter desires. When I first got started, all I had was a 12-volt motorcycle battery, a 100,000-candlepower handheld spotlight (modest by today's standards) and some red cellophane from an auto taillight repair kit, rubber-banded over the lens of the light. It worked just fine.

The sport of night hunting has grown and evolved much since then. These days, there are many products on the market that make night hunting a lot easier and more effective.

Lights

Obviously, a means to see in the darkness is essential for night hunting. I've found that while one handheld spotlight will suffice, a combination of several lights is the ultimate setup. I always wear a battery-powered headlamp. This is not used so much for hunting as it is for small tasks like loading rifles and walking into the calling area. Any good headlamp will suffice. Recently I've been using one of the newer, multiple-LED versions. The bulbs are long-lasting (15,000 hours), and the light is bright enough to walk by as well as take care of small tasks. But it's not so bright that it spreads a telltale glow all over the countryside.

The second necessary light is a handheld spotlight. Something in the million-candlepower range is more than adequate. Over the years, I've used both the internal rechargeable battery types and ones that can be plugged into a remote battery pack. Both have their advantages. The internal-battery models are quick and easy to use. There are no cords to get tangled or extra batteries to carry. The disadvantage of internal-battery lights is that they run out of juice rather quickly. If you're hunting in an area where the calling sessions are short, followed by a drive to a new location – allowing the unit to be charged in the vehicle – they can work fine. But don't expect to get several hours of continuous use out of them without recharging.

Most of the time I use a handheld spotlight with a remote battery pack. These packs are simply an improvement on the old motorcycle battery I carried afield so many years ago. In fact, most of them are motorcycle-type batteries with the addition of a heavy-duty Cordura carrying case and a power receptacle. Some even have a rheostat for adjusting the light's power level. While carrying an extra battery pack means lugging extra weight afield, the advantage is longer life. If you're going to be out for several hours without any means of recharging the batteries for a spotlight, these larger battery packs are the best way to go.

The final light I use is a gun-mounted spotlight atop my riflescope. There are several models currently being made, and I've used several of them. They all seemed to work reasonably well.

A small headlamp is a big help when getting into position, locating items and doing small tasks. The colored LED versions are perfect for these tasks.

There are a couple of big advantages to the gun-mounted spotlight. First, the light points where you're aiming. This seems simple enough, but with one partner working the spotlight and the other shooting, it is often not the case. I've been hunting on several occasions where multiple coyotes came in and my partner was following a different one than I was trying to shoot! Secondly, if you and your partner are sitting close to each other (as you should be), glare from the spotlight tends to reflect from the scope's ocular lens and into your eye — sometimes so much that shooting is impossible (it should be noted that a glare tube can be fashioned from a coffee can or piece of PVC pipe to fit over the end of a handheld light). With a scope-mounted light, the glare is eliminated.

My favorite scope-mounted light has an on/off rocker switch that can be mounted on the rifle forearm for easy access. It also can be powered from a remote battery pack (the same one I use to run a handheld spotlight) or

a smaller battery pack affixed to the butt stock with Velcro straps.

If I'm hunting alone, I use the gun-mounted light for all of my general needs, up until the time of the shot. If I'm hunting with a partner, I bring both the handheld spotlight and the gun-mounted one. The partner glasses with the larger, more powerful light until a predator is in range, then he turns the light off and I shoulder the rifle and switch on the gun-mounted light for the shot.

I always have a red lens cover on the handheld light so it doesn't spook predators. For the gun-mounted light, I prefer a straight white light. Predators can see white light and often stop as soon as it's turned on. As long as you shoulder your gun before turning the light on, you'll usually have a few seconds for a still shot before the animal decides to move off. If I'm using the gun-mounted light by myself, I use a removable red lens. This allows me to "glass" and look for eyes. Then, if I want to stop a predator for a shot, all I have to do is flip off the cover, exposing the white light.

Night Vision Optics

Spotlights work very well for night hunting, but they do have some drawbacks. Using a spotlight can be cumbersome and often requires two people. Further, there's always the possibility of drawing undue attention to yourself. Anywhere I've been night hunting, it was legal to do so. However, it can be inconvenient explaining to area residents or law enforcement officers why you're out in a field at night with a rifle and spotlight. For that reason, in places where there's a good chance others will see the light, I've been experimenting with night-vision optics.

Aside from the different quality levels (which are discussed elsewhere in this book), night vision optics can be broken down in to two main categories. The first are simply optical viewing aids such as monoculars and binoculars. The second are sighting devices complete with adjustable windage and elevation reticles.

For general use, I prefer a monocular or the standard binoculars in place of the handheld spotlight. By surveying the area with night vision optics, it's easy to see a predator coming in to a call (with the help of IR illumination, their eyes glow the same as with a spotlight). When an animal is in range, I flick on the gun-mounted spotlight for the shot. There's hardly any chance of spooking a predator with the light, and area residents don't become alarmed by a spotlight illuminating the night sky.

For more detailed information on Night Vision Optics, refer to the complete section in Chapter 12.

Night Tactics

At night, I often set up in different places than I would during the day. Since visibility is not as great at night, being able to see several hundred yards is not critical. Nor is staying concealed in cover very important. For these reasons, I like to hunt in open fields after sundown. Disked fields lying fallow in the summer and harvested fields such as wheat stubble in the winter are especially productive.

Predators are less reluctant to cross open areas at night because they have little fear of being hunted or caught out in the open. A sage-covered flat or brushy ravine that looks ideal for hunting during the day is often poor at night. Predators will still be there, but being able to see them before they see you is extremely difficult.

I choose my night stands with three key elements in mind. First is easy access. In the dark of the night,

Author with a Western Washington songdog taken at night.

you want to be able to sneak into an area without lots of noise and fuss. If you can negotiate the country without the aid of a headlamp, so much the better. The second key is having an open calling area. This might be a field, natural grassland or a rocky stretch of badlands. In any case, you want to have good visibility for at least 100 yards around your calling position. Finally I like there to be no back door. By this, I mean no easy approach avenue from the rear. In the day, it's easy enough to have another hunter watching the rear, but at night both parties need to remain together looking over a single area.

Night Calling

It would make sense that calling by day and calling by night should be the same. However, this is not true. Night changes the demeanor of most predators; they are more aggressive, more willing to come to a call and will travel longer distances to do so. For these reasons, I call differently at night than I do in the day.

After settling into a stand, I start off my calling sequence with a short burst of mouse squeaks from a bulb-type call, immediately followed by a good scan with a red light. Often coyotes are close at hand, and at night they are not hesitant about responding. If you call too loud and too long, chances are you're either going to scare the critter out of the country or he's going to

Foxes come readily to a call after dark. While they and other predators can be successfully called during the day, this is a bit out of character for them. Night is their true domain.

respond and figure out what's up before you're ready and have a chance to sweep the area with a light.

If nothing comes in on the first series of mouse squeaks, I wait for several minutes and switch to a medium-range cottontail-in-distress call. With this, I call as normal – three series of cries spaced five minutes apart. During this segment, I keep the red light on all the time, pointed at the sky, but so it barely illuminates the foreground for perhaps 50 yards in front of my position. I do this just in case an animal sneaks in while I'm calling. Before I start my next sequence, I lower the red light toward the direction I'm calling and do a complete pan across every area I can see. Then the light goes back up into the air and I start another sequence.

By this time, I've been on stand for roughly 15 minutes, and during the day I would be getting ready to move. At night, however, this is just half the game. At this point, I switch to the medium- or long-range call and really let 'er rip. After one sequence, I generally let out a lone howl (if I'm primarily hunting coyotes). I keep up this routine for the next 15 minutes, the sessions being spaced equally apart in five-minute intervals. Often, a coyote will come during this last 15 minutes.

When I first started night hunting, I thought these late-comers were simply slow to respond, but after watching them approach at a full run and hearing them howl from what seemed to be at least a mile away, I'm convinced that coyotes will travel greater distances at night. This is especially true on a calm winter night. The cold air and frozen ground seems to carry the sound of the call farther and the scarcity of food makes predators even more anxious to fill their bellies – so long-range responses become the norm.

Another difference between calling at night and during the day is the number of multiple animals that will come in. After I shoot a coyote during the day, I continue to call with the hope that another will come in, but I know the odds of that happening are low. That's not the case at night. Stay on your stand after shooting one coyote, and odds are pretty good that another one will come in to the same setup.

Hunting Safely at Night

Any form of hunting has inherent risks, but during the cover of darkness, these risks are magnified. The three main points to remember are: know your target, be sure of your backstop and travel safely to and from your stand.

Knowing your target is the fundamental rule of all hunting, but at night when visibility is decreased, it becomes even more important. All sorts of animals will respond to a predator call. I've had deer, cows, housecats and family dogs all come to calls over the years, so simply seeing eyes is not good enough to make a shot. You need to positively identify what's present before you ever think about firing. *DO NOT ASSUME IT IS A PREDATOR!* This means that most of the time, shots will have to be less than 100 yards.

Even when you're sure the eyes coming into the call are those of a predator, you need to know what lies behind it. Are their cows out there? Are there any buildings? How about a highway off in the distance? The point is, objects so easily identified during the day become invisible at night. For this reason, I only hunt at night in areas where I know the terrain and am very familiar with any possible dangers.

Safety Afield

Firearm safety should always be at the forefront of any hunter's mind, but like all the other aspects of night hunting, the perils of ignoring this rule multiply at night. It's easier to trip and fall while walking to and from stands, which is why I never walk with a chambered round at night and am fully conscience of my muzzle at all times. In addition, it's all too easy to lose track of the exact position of your partner when he's out of sight. Remember the rules of "Zone of Fire" and always err on the conservative side.

It's much better to let a coyote walk than to ever take the slightest risk of injuring something or someone, including yourself.

15

Predator Hunting the Hard Way

Successfully hunting coyotes, foxes or bobcats with archery gear may be the predator hunter's biggest accomplishment.

W hy would anyone want to hunt predators with such short-range weapons as bows, muzzleloaders and handguns? The challenge, of course!

I find predator hunting challenging on any terms, but when I have a bow, muzzleloader or pistol in my hands, the thrill of success is multiplied. The first time I experienced this was in the high elk country of Washington's Cascade Mountains. A partner and I were heading for the trailhead and our waiting truck as the sun dipped below the horizon. From the dark timber far below us, a lone coyote howled. This is not an uncommon occurrence anywhere in the U.S., so we didn't give it much thought. However, several others suddenly answered, and they were much closer. In fact, most were within 100 yards in the ever-darkening timber.

I looked at my partner and quietly asked, "You bring a coyote call?"

Being a Boy Scout by nature, he was always prepared, so it didn't really surprise me when he nodded yes – even though we were strictly hunting elk. We held a quick palaver and decided he would stay put and call while I crept forward another 10 yards to the cover of a small bush. When in position, I nocked an arrow, clipped on my release and gave him a nod.

The squalls of a rabbit-in-distress call cut through the evening stillness. I scanned the timber for movement. Suddenly a coyote came barreling toward us over a rise in the same path we were sitting on. He was running full tilt toward me at about 15 yards when my brain signaled my arms to draw. The coyote immediately caught the movement. Hemmed in by the dense, short trees on each side of the trail, he could not change course, however. His choic-

Author with a coyote that was called into bow range.

Keeping your outline broken and drawing when a predator is out of sight are the two biggest keys to bowhunting predators.

When coyotes are intent on feeding and there's enough cover, they can be stalked with some success, as this one proves.

es were to either keep running toward our gauntlet, or put on the brakes and turn around. Had he kept coming full tilt, there is very little doubt I would have missed him as he blazed by. However, when he saw me, he tried to stop.

His front paws locked straight and he skidded across the ground. He managed to whip a 180 at about the same instant I felt the kisser button touch the corner of my mouth. I'd like to say I picked out a spot and squeezed the trigger, but that would be a lie. As soon as I felt the kisser button, I concentrated on his vitals and punched the trigger. I was immediately relieved to see the arrow disappear where I was looking – it helped that he was only a few feet away! The coyote did a half flip in the air and shot off down the trail. I turned back to my partner and gave him a thumbs up.

My arrow was lodged in the dirt 10 feet from where I hit the coyote, and it was covered with pink, frothy lung blood. We found the 'yote piled up 20 yards down the trail.

To say I was elated would be an understatement – I couldn't have been more proud if I was carrying a 350-class bull elk rack out on my shoulders. OK. Maybe not that proud. My previous close encounters with coyotes had been at around 50 yards, not 3 feet. This was an entirely new rush, and it got me thinking, *Why not practice calling predators extremely close and try to get them with primitive equipment?* The challenge was surely there, and the reward was very satisfying. Since that time, I've shot several coyotes with bows, muzzleloaders and handguns.

Even in rocky, open country, coyotes can be taken with a bow and arrow. A decoy in this kind of terrain works wonders.

Author with two muzzleloader-killed coyotes. Even with a modern muzzleloader like this Knight DISC Extreme .45, shots must be kept within 100 yards.

While at first it seems nearly impossible, with the right techniques and equipment, it can be accomplished.

Archery Gear

The big-game archery equipment you may already own can pull double duty as a predator rig. A standard compound or recurve bow in the 60- to 70-pound range is o more than powerful enough to bring down any coyote. In addition to having enough power, there is another good reason for hunting with your standard big-game bow. It's the same bow you practice with all summer and are proficient with. Hunting coyotes with it in the off-season just gives you more realistic field practice for when that 150-class whitetail steps under your stand.

If you get fanatical about hunting coyotes with a bow and want to have a dedicated setup, here is what I'd suggest: Start with as fast a bow as you can shoot effectively without sacrificing too much in the way of forgiveness and noise. This means that the bow will probably not be operating on the top end of the performance spectrum (300 FPS plus), but will probably be closer to 280 fps.

In addition to having an inherently fast bow, I like to use lightweight carbon arrows. The nice thing about carbon arrows is that they pretty much eliminate the need for an overdraw. You can shoot a full-length carbon arrow, and it will usually weigh close to a shortened aluminum arrow. The longer arrows weigh the same as shorter aluminums, but are more forgiving and easier to tune. All of this adds to the accuracy –needed for a relatively small animal like a fox or coyote.

The next requirement for the perfect predator bow is that it be quiet. Since the speed of sound is roughly three times that of the fastest arrow, the sound generated from a bow will get to a target before the arrow does. On a target made of foam, this is of little consequence. If the target is made of fur, bones and hyperactive reflexes, a sharp twang can make the difference between a solid hit and a complete miss.

There are several silencing methods available, and I tend to err on the conservative side and use many of them in conjunction. For taming limb and riser vibration, I use some of the great products manufactured by Sims' Vibration Laboratories, including Limb Savers. For string and cable noise, I use a combination of Sims' String Leeches and rubber Cat Whiskers. Finally, I cover any exposed metal that could make an untimely clank or bang. The main item is the riser shelf. It only takes one time of having your shaft nick the side of the riser when drawing an arrow on a jacked-up coyote to convince you that padding is needed. Save yourself the frustration and cover this whole region with camo adhesive-backed felt or moleskin.

For sights, I prefer an adjustable, single fiber-optic pin. The large-diameter pin can be readily seen in very low-light conditions. Having only one pin to concentrate on eliminates the chance of picking the wrong pin in the heat of the moment and missing an easy shot. I have learned the hard way that the rule of KISS (Keep It Simple Stupid) applies to predator hunting. In fact, I think Murphy must have been a predator hunter.

The ideal predator archery rig also includes special broadheads. While any broadhead put in the right place will humanely dispatch a coyote-sized animal, I prefer expandable heads for two reasons. At higher velocities, arrow planing can become a problem with fixed heads. It can be overcome, but it seems simpler to avoid it in the first place by using low-profile expandables. Second, most expandable heads provide an extremely large cutting area, which causes massive hemorrhaging and quick death. Some of my favorites include Vortex and Cabela's Terminator opening heads.

Muzzleloaders

Muzzleloaders offer another avenue for primitive predator hunters. Although not as difficult as hunting with a bow, a front-stuffer still provides plenty of challenge.

Any muzzleloader will work. In fact, I shot my first "primitive weapon" coyote with a traditional Thompson/Center Hawken in .54 caliber with a round ball propelled by 60 grains of FFg. Many other hunters use the same rifle they employ for big game for the sense of nostal-

The sport of muzzleloading has come a long way in terms of convenience.

gia as well as for practice.

However, as with archery equipment, some hunters choose to get a dedicated predator muzzleloader. One of the new-generation scope-compatible in-lines is an ideal choice. However, even the most sophisticated in-lines are limited to around 150 yards; most often, they are only 100-yard weapons.

Recently I've been using what might be the ultimate predator muzzleloader: the Knight DISC Extreme in .45 caliber. Originally purchased for antelope and whitetails, this flat-shooting, accurate smokepole is also ideal medicine for coyotes, bobcats and foxes. It fires a polymer-tipped 240-grain bullet with a muzzle velocity of 2,200 fps. This high-ballistic-coefficient bullet retains a lot of velocity and energy at longer ranges. Drop is also minimal, making it a true 150-yard muzzleloader when equipped with a scope. The gun uses the hot #209 shotgun primers, and is also waterproof, making hunting in inclement conditions a real possibility.

Some may argue that such a rifle is not as challenging as using an open-sighted Pennsylvania flintlock with patched round balls. I'd have to concede they are right. But any way you look at it, even the most technologically advanced muzzleloader has only about half the effective range of a modern rifle. Combine this with the fact that there's only one shot and a much slower lock time when compared to a modern rifle, most will have to agree that hunting predators with ANY muzzleloader is a real challenge.

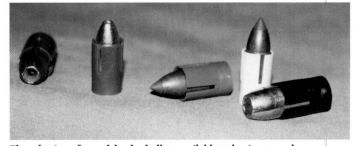

The selection of muzzleloader bullets available today is astounding. This is a small sample of some saboted projectiles.

Handgun Hunting

Depending upon how it's undertaken, handgunning for coyotes can either be almost as difficult as bowhunting or it can be easier than muzzleloading. It all depends on the handgun, as there are both short-range and long-range versions.

Short-Range Handguns

I consider any handgun with an effective range less than 75 yards a short-range handgun. This basically includes all revolvers and automatics. It should be noted I'm referring to field use, by an AVERAGE shooter. It can be argued that in the hands of a truly great shot that a

The Super Blackhawk .44 Magnum as well as other short-range handguns work great on all predators at reasonable distances.

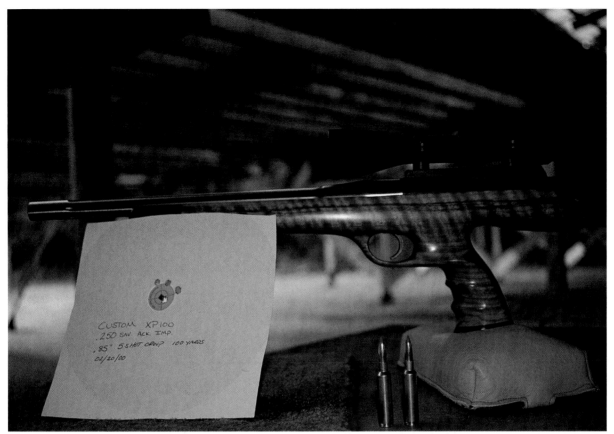

Long-range handguns like this custom XP-100 are capable of riflelike accuracy, as this target shows.

good automatic or revolver can be a much longer-range weapon. However I dismiss this assumption on two premises. First, the cartridges most revolvers and automatics are chambered for are not designed for long-range work. Second, under field conditions, very few shooters have the skill to hit a coyote with one of these weapons much past 50 yards. For most people, revolvers and automatics are short-range weapons.

There is nothing wrong with using a short-range handgun for taking predators. Within their effective range, many have more than enough power and bullet performance to harvest most predators, and the larger calibers have enough energy to harvest any predator. Countless big-game animals ranging from polar bears to Cape buffalo are taken by handgun hunters each year around the world.

The short-range handgun presents a challenge, however. Before an ethical shot can be taken, predators need to be called in close.

Over the years, I've shot predators with close-range handguns ranging from a lowly .22 rimfire in a Browning Buckmark up through a customized 1911 .45 auto, to a long-barreled Ruger Super Blackhawk in .44 Magnum.

It should be noted that some work better than others. For foxes, bobcats and coyotes, I don't recommend anything less than .357 Magnum loaded with rapidly expanding hollow-point bullets. For larger predators such as cougars and bears, I don't recommend anything

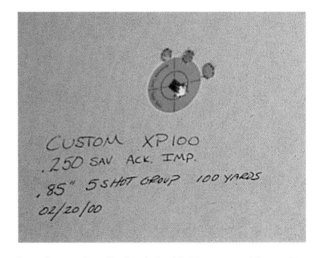

less than a heavily loaded .44 Magnum with quality expanding hunting bullets.

Long-Range Handguns

These fall into a category all of their own. They are more like short rifles than handguns. They are as accurate as most rifles, but are not as easy or convenient to carry as the average handgun. In short, they are a hybrid of rifle and handgun with some of the advantages and disadvantages of each.

Some of the more common are those produced by Weatherby, Thompson/Center (Contender, G4 and

T/C Contenders and the larger Encore are extremely versatile handguns, allowing the user to change barrels from .22 LR all the way up to .45-70.

Encore), Remington XP 100 (the first bolt-action hunting handgun), and more recently the Savage Striker and the HS Precision 2000. All of these guns are serious shooting machines capable of sub-MOA accuracy. When scoped and chambered in the right caliber, these handguns can offer almost the same long-range performance as a rifle.

With short, and consequently stiff, barrels, many are incredibly accurate. I have had experience with several that produced five-shot sub half-MOA groups on a regular basis. This is a hard feat for a rifle, let alone a handgun. But here's the rub: While they are extremely accurate shooting machines, they are hard, physically, to shoot. Although that may seem confusing, it's really simple. The guns are capable of phenomenal accuracy, but it's tough to shoot them under field conditions anywhere near their potential. They can't be shouldered like a rifle, and they really can't be pointed like a pistol with any degree of steadiness. The only option left is to carry a set of shooting sticks, attach a bipod or use natural rests like rocks and tree limbs for support. Any of these can help, but will not be nearly as stable as a rest. I have shot 3-inch groups at 300 yards shooting off a bench rest, but in the field I find that a 150-yard shot on a coyote is tough to make. A lot depends on the individual shooter and how much practice he's willing to invest.

Long-range handguns are available in calibers range from .17 Remington to .45-70, but for most predator

hunting, a pistol chambered in .223, .22-250, .243 or .260 is ideal.

I prefer a variable-powered scope sight, such as the Burris 2x-7x pistol scope. However, for most situations, many handgun hunters agree that a fixed 2- or 4-power can work just fine. It should be noted that there are handgun scopes of higher magnification than 7x. They are hard to use, though, due to their limited eye relief, narrow exit pupil and narrow field of view.

Hunting Techniques for Short-Range Weapons

In order to be consistently successful with a short-range weapon, you must modify your traditional approach to predator hunting. Setups are critical, as is remaining concealed. I avoid any setup where a natural or man-made barrier might prevent a predator from coming into close range. This includes streams, fence lines, brush rows, dirt roads and jagged canyons or dry washes. This is a little bit of a trick since many of these natural features are holding cover and travel corridors for predators (canyons and brush rows, especially) so each setup needs to be examined and judged accordingly.

In addition to avoiding barriers, there has to be an incentive for a predator to close that final gap into range.

Predator hunting with muzzleloaders requires hunters to choose their stands with much deliberation. Before walking into an area, glass it to see if any coyotes are visible.

Before I learned this, I had several hangups occur for no other reason than the coyote could see all of the immediate area around my calling site and found nothing to confirm what his ears were hearing. This can be overcome by two methods: either use a decoy, and/or call from a location that has enough cover to not only conceal you but entices the predator in for a closer look.

Location and available cover is important for all varieties of predator calling, but for the bowhunter, it's paramount. No other method is so limited in range as well as requiring as much physical body movement when the quarry is near. It was this movement that I had the hardest time concealing as a beginner. Here are some tricks that can make a big difference.

A decoy is a great aid to the predator caller, but with a rifle, it's not always required. For bowhunters, however, I feel it's almost a necessity. No other item can direct a predator's attention away from the movements of an archer as well as a moving ball of fur. Used alone, it's not a guarantee of success, though. Several other tricks are almost as important. Call-site selection is vital. Unlike other forms of hunting where concealment is enough, a bowhunter also needs some obstruction to hide the motion of drawing. I have used blinds, both popups and simple screen-mesh varieties and have had mixed results. Pop ups definitely work, but they are hard to transport to and from calling locations. For the multiple setups usually required for predator calling, they simply

take too much time and effort. I prefer to use structures already in the field to conceal my movements.

In rocky badlands, this is relatively easy to do. There are usually numerous boulders, trees, small ridges and cut banks that provide great natural blinds. The key is finding a position that provides a good panoramic view of the surrounding country, but is shielded from close-range inspection by obstructions. Place the decoy in such a manner that it will draw the predator past your shooting position. The trick is to have the bow drawn when the predator comes into range – but not too soon and have to let down due to fatigue. I prefer to watch the coyote approach within 100 yards or less, then, depending upon his speed of approach, duck down behind the cover, draw, anchor and fix my sights on the area where I believe he will reappear. This doesn't always work, but it's the best method I have found. If the coyote is really locked on to the decoy, it may be necessary to stop him with a lip squeak. If you try this, be sure to have your sights on him, finger on the trigger and be ready to shoot. As soon as he turns to look at you, there is generally about a two second window to fire at a stationary target before he realizes what you are and heads for the hills.

I did this on a mousing coyote one time and learned just how fast they can be. He was in knee-high grass, pouncing on rodents. I was downwind, but didn't have a call (I was actually hunting deer), so I started stalking

Every dog has his day. For the author, this handgun-killed coyote took a lot of effort.

him. Every time he put his head to the ground in search of a meal, I'd steal a few paces closer to him. Finally, when I was about 30 yards away and his head was down, I drew, anchored and lined up the sights. His body was pretty much covered by the grass, so I guessed where his head would be and softly whistled through clenched teeth. Immediately his head popped up, right in the middle of the cluster of my sight pins. I centered my 30-yard pin at the juncture of his neck and body, and punched the trigger. As the arrow left the bow, it was like watching in slow motion as his body dropped in an attempt to escape the arrow arching toward him. Luckily it connected with his spine where it met his skull – a good 6 inches above where I'd originally aimed. From the time I whistled until the arrow struck was about a second. Even though I was in full camo standing in the shadows of an aspen grove, he immediately locked on my position and was reacting. Had he been about a tenth of a second faster, or if I'd been a couple of yards farther away, I'd have only hit hair or air.

Always consider man-made objects that may be available. Windmills, water tanks, hay bales, fence corners, old buildings and the like are common throughout good predator country. All can serve as excellent blinds. Many hunters overlook these because they think predators are too wary to go near man-made structures, but this is not true. If an object has been in place any length of time, there is little doubt that every predator in the area has already checked it out both from curiosity and as a source of food, as many small animals and birds live around these sites. I have called from several of these positions with very good luck.

In addition to being very versatile, T/C Contenders are accurate, as this target proves.

16

After the Shot

In the past, one of the main incentives for targeting predators was to harvest pelts the fur market. For many well-known reasons, that market is much smaller than it once was. Yet even today, good-quality pelts have a commercial value and an intrinsic value as trophies and keepsakes. Skull mounts make interesting trophies. Teeth and claws can be turned into attractive primitive jewelry and decorations. These items should not be wasted.

When an inexperienced hunter bags a predator, the first question to come to mind might be, "What do I do now?" The problem may seem overwhelming, especially if the animal is as large as a bear. Skinning, preserving, tanning and mounting trophies are special skills developed through training and experience. The average hunter does not need or desire to become a professional taxidermist, and it's not the intent or scope of this chapter to make him one. The object here is to help you protect your trophy from damage or spoilage until you can deliver it to a taxidermist.

Case Skinning

Case skinning, also called tube skinning, is the most common method of skinning coyotes, bobcats foxes and other small furbearers. The first time I tried this method on a coyote, it took me nearly an hour to remove the hide. When I saw it done by a professional furrier, he completed the job in about 5 minutes. Here's how it's done:

Make a slit down the inside of both back legs. This slit should run from the footpad all the way down to the crotch. If you are doing a standard case skin and don't want to save the feet, now's a good time to remove them. Just slice through the skin all the way around the legs at the ankles. Next, peel the fur away from each leg. At this point, both rear legs will be exposed and the rear hock

Proper field care makes for a much better trophy.

A simple sling made from parachute cord makes carrying a coyote a lot easier.

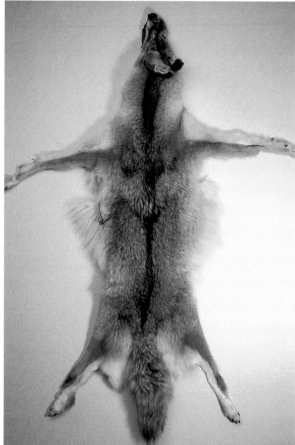

The difference between a case-skinned (left) and flat-skinned (right) coyote.

joint tendons will be visible. Sever the tailbone from the spine at the base. Don't cut through the hide. Removal of the tailbone is described under fleshing and finishing.

From here, the techniques vary. Some hang the animal from a gambrel, hooking it through the tendons, and manually pull the skin away; others use a mechanical aid of some sort. If you have several animals to do, the mechanical-assisted method outperforms the manual method.

Mechanical method: Secure the animal's legs to a solid anchor, such as a tree. Next, take a golf ball and wrap it under the lower edge of the hide. Tie a strong cord over the hide and around the golf ball. Secure the cord to either a come-a-long hand winch or a vehicle ball hitch. With slow, careful pressure, the hide easily peels off. If it sticks or tears the flesh, a little knife work may be needed. Cut through the skin at the front ankles so the front feet can be pulled through the hide (whether skinning manually or with mechanical assistance). The hide will come off without much fuss all the way to where the neck meets the head.

At this point, manual skinning will be needed. Separate the hide from the base of the skull with small cuts and acute pressure. When the ear bases are reached, cut them off as close to the head as possible, leaving the membrane attached inside the ears. Keep skinning toward the nose. The next obstacle is the eyes. From the outside, poke a finger of your non-cutting hand into the eye socket, and pull the facial skin away. The joint between the skull and the eye membrane is now easy to see from the inside. Cut through this membrane, keeping the blade next to the skull and leaving plenty of membrane attached to the pelt. Continue to the corner of the mouth. Using the same method as for the eyes, cut through the membrane and keep working forward, staying along the inner edge of the gum line of the mouth. When the nose is reached, cut through the septum region, leaving the exterior of the nose attached to the pelt.

To flat-skin an animal, start by laying the animal on its back.

Slit the skin from crotch to center of the jaw.

Flat-Skinning

This method applies to any predator to be used either for a rug or a full-body mount. There are some subtle differences between animal species, as well as between a rug or body mount, but the differences are slight and noted in this section. Since bears are the predator most commonly flat-skinned, I will use them as an example.

After shooting a bear, the easiest and surest step to save the quality of the hide is to skin it on site. Work the animal to a relatively flat spot. Roll it onto its back, legs pointing up. All four legs have to be cut, so it really doesn't matter where you start. I like to begin with the back legs. Gripping the rear paw between your legs, make an incision at the rear of the heel (there the pad meets the fur), and run this incision down the inside of the leg to the center of the crotch. Do the same with the other rear leg and the front paws. The two front incisions should meet in the center of the bear's chest.

Now the paws must be cleanly separated from the foot, but must stay attached to the fur. For a rug, cutting a "T" through the center of the pad is the easiest method, since the pad will be removed (and not visible) on the final mount, anyway. For a full-body or shoulder mount, a better, although a little more difficult circumference cut should be used. To do the circumference cut, start at the juncture of the pad and fur, right where the body cut begins, follow this line around the crack between the fur on the side of the foot and the tough pad. Go three-quar-

Make cuts from each paw to the center of the crotch.

Peel back the hide from the belly to the back, using a knife where necessary.

Flesh the skin laying over a smooth board and using an Ulu knife or a specific fleshing knife.

ter of the way around. By sliding the blade of the knife between the fat of the foot pad and the foot bones, the pad can be laid back. Remove the toes from the foot by locating the first joint and sliding the knife blade between, severing the tendons. With the toes removed, the paw, complete with pad attached, can be skinned back down the length of the arm. Do this on all four paws. From the rear crotch where the two leg cuts meet, cut straight up the belly to the center point of the front-leg cuts.

Now the body skinning can commence. Gripping the hide, run a sharp knife between the hide and body. A bear does not have a separating membrane between the skin and flesh as found on deer or elk. The fat and flesh is attached directly to the hide. This makes skinning much more difficult. However, by using a sharp knife and carefully keeping your cuts close to the skin, the hide will come off rather quickly. Remember, the more fat left on the hide, the more work there is to do later and the greater the risk of spoilage and hair slipping. The body can be rolled back and forth to reach the skin over the back.

When you reach the head, remove the skin in the same fashion as previously described in case skinning. The only difference is that it's vitally important not to miscut around the eyes, ears, lips or mouth, as these are all difficult places to patch on a mounted animal. Also be sure to leave plenty of eye, lip and nose interior skin for the taxidermist to work with.

Fleshing and Finish Work

Fleshing is simply removing all shreds of membrane, meat and fat from the hide, the next step after skinning. The best way flesh a hide is to lay it, fur-side down, over a smooth log or board. Take a sharp fleshing knife (such as an Ulu or another knife specifically designed for the task), and begin slicing away the extra fat. Take care to not cut through the hide. Doing the main part of the skin is relatively easy, but once the head is reached, the normal fleshing knife can be exchanged for a small sharp knife (I've used scalpels and Exacto knives, and they worked well). Grab pieces of material to be removed and, while gently pulling, cut them free from the remainder of the hide until all that's left is a smooth, white pelt. This is slow, tedious, messy work, but patience and dedication will help ensure a quality mount.

At this point, the finish work needs to be done on the face. The ears, lips and nose all need to be completely "turned." This entails cutting the dual layers of skin apart to allow salt and air to get in and preserve the skin before the hair follicles can rot, causing the hair to slip out of the skin.

For the ears, start by grabbing onto the cartilage butt, where it was severed from the skull. With a small, sharp knife (an Exacto or scalpel works best here), start cutting between the cartilage and the back skin of the ear. Work this as far down as you can by pulling. After you get about halfway down, the use of a small tool makes the job a lot easier. There are commercial ear-turning tools available. However, a small rounded limb about an inch in diameter by a foot or so long (so it can be grabbed easily) and tapered to a slim, blunt point works great. Simply insert the tapered end into the fur side of the half-turned ear and, while applying pressure, gently cut the cartilage from the skin. This process is slow, but once you get the knack of it, can be accomplished in roughly 15-20 minutes per ear. It's easy to tell when you get the ears all the way turned by feeling from the inside (the fur side) for any unturned portion.

Once the ears are done, the lips must be turned. This is accomplished in much the same fashion as the ears. Start at the cut line where the lips/gums were attached to the jaw. Split the layers down the middle working towards the center of the lip. By keeping your fingers of your non-cutting hand on the outside of the lip, it's relatively easy to determine when the lip is fully split. It will feel like one continuous piece of hide with no lumps inside. Work all the way around from the corner of the mouth to the front of the lips, making sure to split their entire length.

The meat and vertebra must be pulled out of the tail to prevent spoilage and hair slipping. The simplest way is to use a product called a "tail puller." Make a small incision at the base of the tail, grip the meaty portion and bone inside, and begin skinning it away from the fur. When a couple inches are free, grab it with the puller and while gripping the furred portion, pull. This works best on a fresh pelt. If the tail does not come out, the best bet is to manually skin it by splitting the tail straight along the bottom. This can later be sewn up to hide the incision.

After all the skinning and preparation work is done, it's time to preserve the pelt. For a coyote, fox or other small case-skinned animals, this can be as simple as stretching the hide (fur side in) over a stretcher (available in commercial form or made by trimming a board to size) and left to air-dry. In areas with a damp environment, a dusting or powdered Borax will aid in preservation and drying. For a larger animal such as a bear, spread the hide out, fur side down, and salt the skin. Be sure to coat the entire skin. Do not miss any folds and pack all openings of paws, ears, eyes, lips and nasal passage with a liberal amount of salt. Once thoroughly covered, fold the head back onto the skin, the legs back into the center, and roll it up like a sleeping bag. Let the salt penetrate the hide for approximately 24 hours, then unroll and hang it by the head to let the excess brine run off. Let it drain for another 24 hours and then repack it in salt and reroll it. It should keep well until you can get it out of the field. If not going to a taxidermist right away, keep it in a freezer to further preserve the skin.

Turn the lips, ears and pull the claws so they don't spoil and ruin the mount or rug.

Care of Skulls

The skull from a predator makes a unique trophy, and in the case of a bear or cougar, is the actual item for book measurements and entry. When cleaned, whitened and mounted, it makes a great keepsake and can provide many memories of a successful hunt. Another advantage is that skull processing is relatively simple and can be done by the hunter with minimal experience, cost or equipment.

Sever the skull from the body by locating the juncture between the first vertebra and the actual skull. This joint can be a little tricky to find, but by probing with the point of a sharp knife, it can be located with a little effort. Once found, cut through all the exterior tissue and work the blade in between the two bones, severing the spine. While twisting the skull, keep cutting until it's free from the carcass. The next step can be done at home or in the field, but I prefer to do it in the field as the scraps can be easily discarded. Starting at the top of the skull, fillet the main muscle groups away from the skull working down toward the inside of the jaw. Simply keep the blade next to the bone and keep peeling away flesh. When the main muscles are removed, cut the bottom skin and tongue free from the jaw. At this point spend a few more minutes, cutting away as much of the remaining flesh and tissue as possible.

Once stripped, the skull is ready for the final steps which can done at home or by a taxidermist. If you choose to do it yourself, there are excellent kits available from Van Dykes Taxidermy or Cabela's that have all the chemicals and instructions needed to obtain professional-looking results. These kits contain enough material for several skulls.

Manufacturer Listings

Advanced Decoy Research
Manufacturer of the Predator
Supreme Decoy and the All-Call
3760 Forrest Hill Road
Bolivar, TN 38008
Phone (731) 658-2934
www.decoyheart.com

Burnham Brothers Game Calls
Predator call innovator and manufacturer since 1952. Founded by
predator hunting pioneer Murry
Burnham.
P.O. Box 427
Menard, TX 76859
(915) 396-4572
www.burnhambrothers.com

Cabela's
Simply put – Everything under the
sun.
One Cabela Drive
Sidney, NE 69160
(800) 237-4444
www.cabelas.com

Johnny Stewart
Predator call manufacturer since
1961. Well-known and respected for
its innovative electronic calls.
6000 Hunting Court Northeast
Cedar Rapids, IA 52402
(800) 537-0652
www.hunterspec.com
jswc@hunterspec.com

Kahles
Makers of fine optics
2 Slater Road
Cranston, RI 02920
(401) 734-5888
www.kahlesoptic.com

Kimber
Fine-rifle manufacturer
1 Lawton St.
Yonkers, NY 10705
(406) 758-2222
www.kimberamerica.com

Knight Rifles
Muzzleloader manufacturer
21852 Hwy. J46
Centerville, IA 52544
(641) 856-2626
www.knightrifles.com

Leupold & Stevens, Inc.
American-made fine optics
14400 Northwest Greenbrier Pkwy.
Beaverton, OR 97006
(503) 646-9171
www.leupold.com

Outland Sports
Makers of Feather Flex Decoys and
Lohman predator calls
4500 Doniphan Dr.
Neosho, MO 64850
(417) 451-4438
www.outland-sports.com

Primos Hunting Calls
Known for their good selection
of mouth-blown predator callers
604 First Street
Flora, MS 39071
(800) 523-2395
www.primos.com

Raw Calls
The finest manufacturer of custom
predator calls
1120 Pasadena Place
Sidney, NE 69162
(308) 254-7064
E-mail: *rawcalls@hotmail.com*

Remington Arms Co., Inc.
Manufacturer of muzzleloaders,
rifles and ammunition
870 Remington Drive
Madison, NC 27025-0700
(800) 243-9700
www.remington.com

Robinson Laboratories, Inc.
Scent-elimination products and
activated-carbon clothing
110 North Park Drive,
P.O. Box 18,
Cannon Falls, MN 55009-0018
(507) 263-2885
www.robinsonlabs.com
E-mail: *info@scentshield.com*

Swarovski
Makers of fine optics
2 Slater Road
Cranston, RI 02920
(401) 734-5888
www.swarovskioptik.com

**Trophy Mountain Outfitters/Dean
Silva**
Excellent Colorado guide service,
offering first-rate trips for coyotes
and bobcats
tmohunt@yahoo.com
(719) 580-0788

Winchester Firearms
Manufacturer of muzzleloaders,
rifles and ammunition
275 Winchester Ave.
Morgan, UT 84050
(801) 876-3440
www.winchester-guns.com

Weatherby
Fine-rifle manufacturer
3100 El Camino Real
Atascadero, CA 93422
(805) 466-1767
www.weatherby.com